THE SINGING BIRD WILL COME

Living With Love, Strength, and Joy

by

Dionne C. Blaha

THE SINGING BIRD WILL COME

Living With Love, Strength, and Joy

by

Dionne C. Blaha

PARKSIDE Publishing Corporation

205 West Touhy Avenue
Park Ridge, Illinois 60068

Copyright © 1992 Parkside Publishing Corporation

All Rights Reserved. No part of this book may be reproduced or transmitted in any form or by any means, electronic or mechanical, including photocopying, recording, or by an information storage and retrieval system without express permission in writing from the publisher. Printed in the United States of America.

0 1 2 3 4 5 6 7 8 9 10

The Singing Bird Will Come

Illustration by Dionne C. Blaha

ISBN 0-942421-47-7

This book and I might have remained dormant for many more years without the help of my able therapist, Ann Veilleux. I also thank my former writing teachers Bev Jonnes and Ron Wallace for having gone out of their way to encourage me. And I thank my lucky stars because acknowledging former teacher Terry Spohn meant finding he'd become an editor who happened to be looking for books like this one. My appreciation goes especially to him for his assistance in helping this book happen.

*If I keep a green bough in my heart,
the singing bird will come.*

Chinese Proverb

CONTENTS

Introduction	1
One: Where Did We Come From?	3
Two: Daily Victories	13
Three: Acting Outside of "Shoulds"	19
Four: Journey to the New	27
Five: The Kindness of People	35
Six: Gathering Self-Protection	49
Seven: Asserting Consumer Rights	61
Eight: Being Seen	69
Nine: Living in the Body	81
Ten: Assertiveness in Relationships	91
Eleven: Sex and Intimacy	103
Twelve: Assertiveness at Work	115
Thirteen: Major Life Changes	125
Fourteen: Prosperity and Deservedness	137
Fifteen: Today and Tomorrow	145
Appendix A: What Might Have Happened?	149
Appendix B: Traps To Watch For	151
Appendix C: Am I The Only One?	153
Appendix D: What Do I Feel During Sex?	157
Postscript	161

Introduction

If you are an incest survivor, or believe you are, welcome to an exploration of your self. It can be a short trip or an extended one, however you like it. Either way, you may discover something inspiring you didn't know.

I have not studied the topic of incest from an academic point of view. Because I am a survivor, I have discovered how heavy the mud of incest issues can be. I have struggled with my levels of self-esteem and sexual awareness, and I have discovered how to remold my personality so that I can take pride in who I've come to be. Because my primary issues have revolved around a sense of powerlessness, internalized blame and shame, spiritlessness, and isolation, this book is particularly for you if you find it difficult to figure out your needs, have trouble voicing what you feel or think, or feel unworthy of healthy attention from others.

For a survivor, reading books about incest can be just another harrowing experience. None of us wants to relive the terror and abandonment of the past. That's why even considering reading a book about incest can fill us with a sense of dread and keep us from doing it.

This book is not intended to push you into reliving any part of your abuse. The scariest part asks us to risk little more than a new point of view. It does not encourage us to do anything we are not ready to try. In this way, this book is about personal choices. (Incidentally, I have chosen to use both pronouns "she" and "he" throughout the text to include all survivors of incest.)

New understanding comes to us especially when we talk to others and read books. In doing so we risk opening a door we have kept closed or haven't even seen for a long time. On the other side of that door might be a sky full of soothing blues, or the smell of rain, or the first singing bird in the early morning trees. But we can't know the possibilities without opening the door.

To be still and frightened is part of our sad past. Welcome to the chance to widen your own horizons, to begin opening your eyes a little more every day.

1

Where Did We Come From?

*The past is a foreign country;
they do things differently there.*

L.P. Hartley

How far we have come since we lived under the shadow of incest! It took some of us many years before even the vaguest memories began to occur for us. Perhaps we finally realized that the uncomfortable things done to us were actually criminal acts. Since those moments of realization, we have encountered a bewildering number of feelings. They've ranged from shock that this was indeed incest and denial that this ever affected us, to disappointment and disbelief that our family life was not as positive as we believed. We have cried when we realized we never had the chance for a free and easy childhood, and we felt angry when we began to know how many wrong ideas we'd been given about life, love, trust, and sex. A feeling that persisted underneath all these was our deep sense of isolation and aloneness.

As we've progressed, we've begun to discover that we are not as alone anymore. We are living in a time when we hear the stories of others in newspapers, books, and movies. It remains true that the less we are isolated, the more we can heal. To that end, this book's purpose is to help us to further know ourselves so that we are better able to choose healthier lifestyles and warmer connections with others.

The Burden of Abuse

As we know, it has been a challenging and often difficult process to find our way out from under the shadow of incest. It has been complex for more than one reason. Whether abusive adults are conscious of it or not, they tend to use three ways to keep a child suppressed. They teach the child self-destructive ways to think about herself, rules she cannot free herself from. These adults often fail to accept or even recognize feelings the child has, except to reinforce and manipulate those of shame and guilt. And finally, they may support her needs with a confounding inconsistency, use her needs against her, or act as though her needs do not exist at all.

These destructive ways of thinking, unknown feelings, and unidentified needs remain part of the child. He or she carries them into adulthood, and each of them shows up in everyday behaviors. Conversely, those who grow up in a supportive family atmosphere have a different level of trust and confidence and this is revealed in their daily decisions.

There is nothing bad or wrong with the limited ways we may be living our lives. The fact that we survived at all is remarkable. (For an idea of the obstacles we defeated, see Appendix A at the back of this book.) Our goal is to take a new look at our limits and make sure they are still what we want for ourselves. To that end, our behaviors can be seen as symptoms, or flags, for what lies underneath. For example, we may not initially understand why we tend to walk down a city street looking only straight ahead or at the sidewalk, not even glancing into store windows. But when we make note of the behavior, we might also remember that our body feels like "plowing ahead" or maintaining a kind of tunnel vision during those situations. We may then be stimulated to recall a similar feeling when we're in a car waiting next to other cars—we don't look at the other drivers or passengers. The feelings which initially guided us to do these things this particular way may be infused with shame and confusion. This is why, at least for now, it can be more helpful to view our behaviors as flags until we naturally begin to associate a certain behavior with a certain way of feeling.

As another kind of example, suppose you are driving in an unfamiliar part of a city and you get lost trying to find a friend's house. Or perhaps you're in a large supermarket and cannot locate an odd item like pickled herring. Do you keep on looking, or do you ask someone for directions?

Perhaps you ask for assistance right away. Perhaps you keep trying until you're sure you can't do it on your own, and then you ask. Or you might not ask at all.

While a confident person has little difficulty interrupting a clerk or passerby and asking for help, it is not such a simple task for most incest survivors. Inherent in our abuse was the reinforcement of dependence on the family which was intensified by our feeling of powerlessness. In some, this dependence remains chronic through adulthood. It may prompt automatic reliance on strangers as well. However, for most of us our deep feeling of inadequacy is obscured by our even deeper mistrust of others. This means silence usually wins out in the end.

Old Lies

These are simply the effects of our training. What were some of the things we were made to understand? Sometimes simply reading statements like the following can be enlightening because we suddenly recognize one that deeply affects our lives. Feel free to write down any others you remember or change the language until they are just like the ones you heard. Listen to the lines, but be careful not to soak in the confusion they generate, since their original intent was to provoke shame in us.

Don't trust anyone. Other people are out to get you.

Stick to yourself. Nobody else can help you.

Keep quiet and do it yourself—it makes you stronger and independent, makes you learn things.

You're the only one here who doesn't know what they're doing. Everyone else knows how.

If you say anything, you are going to look stupid!

Besides, you should know better. Where did you come from, a cave?

You got yourself into this, you gotta get yourself out.

Next time you'll be more careful, won't you?

These kinds of statements are part of the makeup of emotional abuse. They include shaming comments, black-and-white (all-or-nothing) thinking, and false beliefs. They also include a flipping kind of logic that suits the speaker, as when a parent attacks a child's powerlessness ("You mean you don't know how to do that yet?") and later gives the child far too much control and power ("Don't make me get angry at you."). These assertions serve to keep the child off-balance and insecure. They are crazy-making.

These statements, when internalized, severely retard a child's emotional growth. In fact, many people remain emotionally crippled for the rest of their lives. None of these kinds of life lessons is filled with compassion, help, or recognition.

New Ways

Now let's take another look. What would have happened if we had been told the following things instead?

> *Go ahead and ask that person for some directions. If you get stuck, I'll be right here to help you out.*
> *Did you know?—it's actually part of his job to help you!*
> *If she seemed rude, it's not because of anything you did—she may just be having a bad day.*
> *Everyone asks for directions sometimes.*
> *You haven't been here to see the people who have asked for help, but I'll bet this person has given out help several times already today.*
> *It can be distressing to be lost, or to waste a lot of time trying to find something, but there are ways to get help.*
> *Few people enjoy being lost.*
> *We'll find our way together next time too, won't we?*

What a different way to show us the world! Being helped with these kinds of encouraging statements would certainly have fostered trust and connection with others.

In the chapters ahead we will take a look at some behaviors and ways of thinking and then ask ourselves if they make us feel as good as we would like to feel.

The goal is not to push us into doing everything differently, which is a paralyzing thought in itself. The goal is to take a different point of view for a moment, to look through a clearer pair of eyes, to help us answer the question, "Is the shadow of abuse winning, or am I?"

I can change how I feel about myself.

2

Daily Victories

Live the questions now.
Perhaps you will gradually, without noticing it,
live along some distant day into the answer.

Rainer Maria Rilke

How To Use This Book

There are many suggestions listed in the following chapters. Remember that these ideas are intended to be for you and in your best interest, not another job to do. If one item stops being fun or inspiring, exercise a different choice or put the book down for a while.

You won't need to do most or even half of the suggestions listed. Many will not be suited to you. Even though they are stated as directives, you don't have to do any of them. Just reading them and letting them rest in your memory is a perfect thing to do.

The items are identified by risk level and a corresponding number of stars. One-star items are a good starting place for that chapter's particular issue, and two- and three-star items represent gradually-increased levels of risk. Keep in mind that these are merely estimations of risk, nothing more. If you find you are already accomplishing an item with ease, use this generalized scale as a measure of what you are already good at and which direction to take next. You may not have realized how many risks you already take in a day. Be sure to take credit for what you're already accomplishing!

Some of the suggestions overlap from chapter to chapter, which is not accidental: many of our issues overlap the same way. Also, the chapters progress somewhat in their level of risk, so it may not be as gentle to begin with later chapters. As we proceed, we may be surprised to find we keep falling into certain emotional or mental traps left over from our past. These pitfalls, such as our nagging voice of inadequacy, can prevent us from progressing if we're not conscious of them. (More of these are listed in Appendix B, "Traps to Watch For.")

Most of the suggestions apply both to women and men and if they do not, they are so noted. Some of the suggestions you can do on your own at any time you choose. Others will address choices you can make when something outside your control occurs, as when you are in a public place around other people.

More Questions

While the items in the chapters are succinctly stated, any of them can be a springboard for further questions. For example, perhaps we are reading a chapter about our increasing level of comfort while feeling visible. An item might suggest we look briefly at the face of one more stranger than we did yesterday. Considering doing this item might prompt us to ask ourselves, "How many strangers did I look at yesterday, anyway?" "How do I normally look at people—do I avoid all strangers, or only those of a certain sex?" "Do I tend to glance away, stare them down, or do I like to greet them with my eyes?" "Does my curiosity about who they are supercede my fear of unknown people?" "Will it bother me to try doing this?" "Why have I been doing things this way, anyway?"

These and other gently probing questions might be generated by any item. The most important question to ask ourselves is, "Am I happy with how I do this?" It can be enlightening to hear ourselves say "no" to this. Knowing this becomes a starting point for changing how we do something. When we say "yes" to this question, we can feel satisfied that we have developed one more area of our lives.

As incest survivors, we have ways of doing certain things to help us feel safe in what used to be an unsafe world. The ideas that follow are not intended to take away from our sense of security. In fact, quite the opposite. If we are limited in certain important ways, we most likely cannot feel as fulfilled in our life as we could, or very well linked with others. These ideas, if practiced in a gradual way, will increase our confidence in our abilities. And every single step we take is a victory.

With each step I make, I claim my power.

3

Acting Outside of "Shoulds"

Throw away all thoughts of imaginary things, and stand firm in that which you are.

Kabir

After a lifetime of adherence to ways of thinking imposed by others, it may be hard for us to begin to break out. It will help if we start with a general issue so we can adjust to new attitudes about ourselves. The ideas in this chapter, therefore, act as "basic training." Learning positive self-talk will help us lay the groundwork for meeting more specific challenges later.

Let's Begin

Sometimes we do things automatically to avoid brushing against feelings of shame. This most often occurs when we are in the presence of others. During these times, we are often "outside of our bodies" because we are busy worrying about how others are judging us.

Since we may be aware of how our friends or spouse think of us, let's address the standards of people we haven't communicated with. We tend to imagine lots of standards strangers might have. It is the question, "What will they think of me?" that keeps us acting in accordance with what we think might be "correct." And what a mess of guessing that can get to be!

This topic includes a second part about intrusive strangers—people who are doing something that is bothersome. These two issues are similar because they are an exercise in holding onto our own reality in the face of another's.

Both sections are about becoming aware of the "shoulds" we imagine strangers to hold over us. These include thoughts we have such as,

They don't want me to waste their time (by being in line in front of them, by contesting a sales slip just rung up, or by writing down my gas mileage before paying for my gas).

They think I shouldn't be so picky about selecting this product. I should be satisfied with it as it is.

They are judging me right now (for buying too many unhealthy foods, because I don't look attractive, or because I act clumsy).

Remembering Who We Are

It may help you to realize that any imagined "should" is just as arbitrary as any other imagined "should." That's why it's a good idea to entertain a different one, or the opposite one. For example, if you normally don't like to take too long at the local drive-in bank when someone is behind you, take a minute more than usual to fill out your slip carefully, and pretend the people behind you aren't thinking poorly of you but are using that time to fill out their deposit slips or read a newspaper.

A question that can help clarify your real wants is, "If I were totally alone in this situation, would I be doing exactly this same thing?" Here are some things to try:

★ When you go to a grocery store or a farmer's market, be more selective than usual when picking out your fruits and vegetables. Put back anything with a bruise or a cut.

- ★ Take a day to eat exactly what you want, exactly when you want.
- ★ When you're packing a suitcase or overnight bag, pack it with as many things as you want.
- ★ When buying a newspaper from a stack, if the top one is mis-folded or looks beat-up, take the second one. And if the top one looks good, pick the second one just for practice.
- ★ Discover as much play time as you want, and spend it playing cards, doing crosswords, or fixing jigsaw puzzles.
- ★ Let's say you go to a public library or bookstore because you're in the mood for a romance novel or any other topic that makes you feel exposed or even a little ashamed. Pick out as many books as you want.
- ★ To become more aware of how attitudes are reinforced, look at magazines, listen to the radio, or watch television and identify one or more advertisements that show a person disapproving of another or shaming or

pointing a finger at someone for having any one of the following "conditions." (Also, identify any euphemisms or shaming slogans that stigmatize these conditions like calling hand freckles "age spots" or a woman having a "not-so-fresh" feeling.)

sweat
static electricity in clothes or hair
warts
sneezing from allergies
feminine smells
skin blemishes
dandruff
freckles on hands
overweight
untidy bathroom
dry skin
stains on clothes

⋆⋆ When a restaurant serves you an excessive portion, eat what you want and ask for the rest to be wrapped to take home.

⋆⋆ Turn up the radio in your car, and with the windows up or down, sing with a bit of gusto.

- ★★ At a grocery store, if you discover you have a grocery cart that squeaks or tracks to one side, take it back and trade it for a better one.
- ★★ When you are driving the speed limit and can't find a house or store you are looking for, slow down a little even if someone is right behind you.
- ★★★ If you are handing food stamps to a cashier, try handing them over freely like money, without hiding them from others.
- ★★★ Find a dance room to go to, and dance how you want.
- ★★★ During a sad movie in a theater, try letting a few tears fall down your cheeks.

Asserting Ourselves

We are occasionally in situations where someone is rude or bothering us. Being unused to asking for our rights often makes us keep quiet about these things. We are used to rationalizing by saying to ourselves, "I can live with this. I'm not dying, after all, and things could be worse."

A good question to ask yourself is, "Do I wish this situation would just go away?" If you want, imagine you are taking the role of an assertive person you know. Here are some ways we can practice being more assertive:

★ You are driving behind a car that brakes suddenly several times for no apparent reason, then turns off the road without using a turn signal. Honk your horn as you pull around the driver.

★ While in a public place you see someone verbally harassing or roughly treating another person. Simply acknowledge to yourself that, regardless of this person's intentions, you still feel this is abusive behavior.

★★ You were next in line. Someone is either trying to slip in front of you, or the sales help is calling on others first. Step forward and say you're next.

★★★ Some people are noisy behind you in a movie theater, disrupting your enjoyment of the film. Turn and ask them to be quiet.

★★★ Let's say you can't concentrate, or perhaps fall asleep, because of a neighbor's noise, whether it is loud music, hammers pounding, or a sander on a car. Ask him what hours he's planning on working and see if he can compromise on the hours you need to work or sleep. In case he refuses, by, for example, saying he has a deadline to meet, either press further by stating you also have work to complete, or accept that he will be done soon and ask him when he estimates he'll be finished.

While these are specific examples, others may arise that you used to avoid and that you now realize have always carried a risk factor for you. Look at them as opportunities you can recognize, and this time, instead of turning away, remember that you can choose what you want to do about them.

I like discovering how I want to live my life.

4

Journey to the New

In times of change, learners inherit the earth, while the learned find themselves beautifully equipped to deal with a world that no longer exists.

Eric Hoffer

Building Confidence

How do people gain confidence? Certainly, babies are not born feeling independent and capable. No one grows confident without the benefit of gentle encouragement and positive reinforcement.

One of the ways we build confidence is through exposure to many different situations. It not only hones our capabilities, it also informs us about our real strengths. Along the way it is natural to stumble occasionally, but as we proceed, and if we are determined enough, we can let fears prevent us less and less from doing things we would like to.

No one ever becomes perfect at trying new things, because "new" means different from anything we've seen before. No one is adept at throwing a frisbee the first time, or finding the way to a park in the middle of a strange city.

Though the things we try may be different, certain skills begin to transfer from one task to the other, such as the ability to read a map, which can help us locate anything from a party at a friend's house to a waterfall along a hiking route. Another useful skill is the ability to understand others' directions. We soon learn about other people's skill at seeing the terrain through a newcomer's eyes, how they organize their thoughts, and how they transfer their ideas to us in words. Learning effective questions that will clarify instructions can save us much frustration and time. This is an example of how a risk may have several levels of difficulty. You may gather your courage to ask a person where your turnoff is, and he or she answers, "Just down this road, past the next stoplight." At this point you can thank him or her and be on your way, or you can save yourself miles of wondering by asking further questions like, "How far is it to the stoplight? And how far beyond the stoplight is the turnoff?" You might have thought it was a few blocks away, and the native knows it's four miles down the road.

By clarifying instructions you ensure you will meet your party on time or that your cake won't fall. Asking effective questions can guarantee that you are paying for the particular product you had in mind.

While reading some of the following items, you may feel a level of discomfort if some of them seem too scary. Start with just one item, one that is a little challenge for you but that you know you can do. If you succeed in doing it in the next couple of days, congratulate yourself! Reward yourself by doing something you enjoy, like reading a book you just signed out from the library, playing a board game with a friend, or watching a movie you've wanted to see. It may be helpful to remember that even the reward you choose was new to you once. You had to take a risk to try it that first time. You might find any of these items equally enjoyable.

Risks to Begin With

- ★ Think of an area near home or on the way home that you would like to explore. Drive down a different street and look at what's there. For a little higher risk, take a bike ride or walk through an area that's new to you.
- ★ Take a walk down a grocery aisle you usually skip. You can also look on the shelves until you see an item you've never noticed before. Notice what it looks like, its style and colors.
- ★ Pick a new washer at your laundromat and do your clothes there, or sit in a new area.
- ★ When you go to the grocery store, buy a food item you normally buy in a brand you haven't tried yet.
- ★ When you walk into class, pick a new chair and sit there for today.
- ★ Even if you've tried plant care but had no

success before, bring a new plant into your living or work space. Admire it from time to time.

- ★ Order a dish you haven't tried when you go to a restaurant.
- ★ Buy a beginning plumbing book to refer to when making minor repairs on your own.
- ★ Buy one new food that you've never bought before.
- ★ At a mall, walk into one store you usually pass by.
- ★★ When a friend invites you to do something with him or her that you've never tried but have wanted to do, say yes. (Tell your friend about your nervousness, if you want to. That's a two star risk also!)
- ★★ Find a new beach and go there to read a book or write a letter, or even go swimming.
- ★★ Go to a second-hand shop. Look around and see if there's anything interesting.

- ★★ Find your way to a new movie theater to see a film.
- ★★ Go to a different library. Find the card catalog and any other section you want, like the magazines or newspaper rack.
- ★★ When you are at a clothing store, try on (with no intention of buying) an article of clothing that you haven't tried on before. See if it looks different than you imagined, or better than you thought it would.
- ★★ Find a new restaurant to try.
- ★★ When a friend invites you to meet in an unfamiliar location, accept if you want to. Ask for directions on how to get there, and, if necessary, where to find parking.
- ★★ Go into a shop and buy something for yourself when you feel like it.
- ★★ Buy a small article of clothing, like underwear or socks, that is even just a little different than the kind you're used to.

★★ Select a hobby you've wanted to try for some time but didn't know how. With the intention of doing only this step, go to a bookstore or library and get a book about it. Don't pressure yourself to read the book or get started in any other way. Just leave the book out, and if and when your curiosity comes up, you'll have something to feed it with.

★★★ Find a new night spot you can go dancing in.

★★★ Enroll in an interesting mini-course at a local college.

★★★ Locate a state park you've not gone camping in and go there with a trusted friend to spend a night or two in a tent.

★★★ Think of a new activity you've wanted to try for a long time, like horseback riding or going to a state fair. Figure out a way to do it, either alone or with a friend.

★★★ Pick a place you could drive to, either by yourself or with a friend, and plan a weekend, or a week-long trip to take an adventure.

The possibilities are endless. Their numbers don't scare us as much when we realize their sole purpose is for us to enjoy them. As the mists of fear dissipate, we realize there is a whole world lying at our feet, just waiting to be discovered.

I feel good about myself when I try new things.

5

The Kindness of People

What loneliness is more lonely than distrust?

George Eliot

Many of us find it difficult to ask for what we need. Sometimes it's easier to confront a stranger, sometimes a friend. Sometimes we don't ask at all.

Why did we ever stop asking for help from others? Many of us appealed to someone in our most urgent time of need and went unheard. For many of us, one of the only persons who was supposed to be dependable was hurting us. Many of us were even punished for saying our needs out loud.

Incest survivors, on the whole, have reservoirs of independence to draw from when independence seems called for. We think, "I did it alone all my life," and so we continue.

But at what cost? How much extra time do we spend because of our determination to see something through on our own? At times we cultivate a stubbornness that forms a fortress around us. At what point are we losing out?

We lose when we don't have as many friends as we want. We don't win when the quality of our relationships is hurtful or simply not quite as good as it could be. And we don't triumph like we might if we could allow ourselves to depend on someone else for something now and then.

'Dependence' is a word that makes many people uncomfortable. But dependence and powerlessness need not be synonymous. As adults, when we begin asking for help, we feel our own vulnerability. We recognize we are not superhuman. Ironically, to have humility takes strength. It means we trust ourselves enough to experience the insecurity of releasing our control.

Building Bridges Instead of Walls

To be in control might give us an illusion of safety, but it is only an illusion. If our skills remain unborn, we have to cover that with rigidity and an isolation we might mistakenly call independence. Maintaining a kind of rigidity, standing behind a wall of control, is a way of remaining fragile. If an arrow pierces that thin wall, it pierces us also, for we have no protection for our soft interiors. While we might wish we were shielded like a clam with two shells to keep out intruders, we as humans have to find other ways to protect our soft skin and tender feelings. Our protection comes in the form of tools and skills. When we develop the skills every person needs in an ever-changing environment, we can begin to relax. Our feeling of safety increases when we learn how to share intimately with others and how to stand up to anyone who threatens us.

Releasing a little of our control means learning how to be more honest with ourselves by admitting when we could use assistance and by owning the fear we have about asking. It also means finding out how to communicate effectively with others by gathering information from them when we need it. Let's make up a specific example. Pretend you want a certain cassette tape of Cajun music. You've looked in many music stores and you haven't been able to find it. Eventually you figure it's not available and soon you forget about looking anymore.

In another scenario, in your first store or two, you question a clerk on its availability. He says, "Yes, we do have it. Maybe it's not on the shelf, but I have one in the back." When he returns with two tapes in his hand, he says, "If you like that group, have you heard of this one? This group does the same kinds of songs, but I like this one even better." For the one risk you took, you have been rewarded twice.

People Are Resources

Just as you do for them, people tell you what certain words mean, what direction to take, what an item has to offer. They may even tell you a valued secret of theirs, like which fish market has the best shrimp, how they've noticed an inferior feature on this particular telephone answering machine, or where to find the grandest array of flowering plants. Some of these ideas you'll take their advice on, and they'll turn out to be gems you never forget.

Of course, the reason we fear asking people questions is not that they won't know an answer, but how they will answer. We fear rejection, or unfriendliness. We are gun-shy. As children, we learned not to trust, but it's time to wonder if there might be some friendly people out there in the world.

First, we can ask ourselves, "Does the sight of every stranger make me a little anxious?" Because we were abused by someone with that same kind of physical shape, chances are that we generalized our fear of our perpetrators onto all human beings. That looming fear of the unknown and fear of someone's possible authority or aggressiveness can be triggered when we see any stranger coming toward us. In light of this, it's a good idea to reassure ourselves of who is really out there by saying to ourselves, "This person is not my father (or mother, or brother, etc.)."

Another helpful idea is to practice surrounding yourself with an imaginary protector, like an imaginary blanket or a tunnel of white light sheltering you. The purpose of this protection is to remind you of your boundaries. Like your skin, these boundaries act like a mirror whenever someone tries to dump something unfavorable on you. But your blanket or circle is receptive to the friendliness of others, and you can return your response to them through it, too. See what it feels like to really take in a smile, instead of having it bounce off you, off the old wall of rigidity. Sometimes a warm smile is all it takes to make your day.

Be sure to assign the helpful answers you receive just as much weight as any negative responses. Chances are that you will receive sixty to ninety-five percent friendly responses.

Asking Help From Strangers
- ★★ Ask someone on a city street what time it is.
- ★★ Call a theatre for movie times.

    Note: If using the telephone makes you feel nervous, start by calling your local weather forecast and other message recordings, the numbers for which can be found in your telephone directory. Then, when you begin to call people, it's helpful to jot down your questions, even word-for-word if you want to, on a piece of paper.

- ★★ Call a store or post office or your bank to find out what their hours are.
- ★★ To familiarize yourself with some of the organizations that exist just to serve you, look in your telephone book's yellow pages under Human Services Organizations and Social Service Organizations.
- ★★ Call for the price of an item at a store. Call another store to compare prices.
- ★★ Find the phone number for your Social Security Administration office under the U.S. Governmental section entitled Health

and Human Services. Call this office to find out where to get a form to verify your social security wages to date (a procedure worth doing every three years).

★★ Go to an information booth at a mall or a fair, and stop to ask a question.

★★ If you are a renter, and a fixture in your apartment stops working or something else is in need of repair, call your rental manager and ask to have it fixed.

★★ Ask for directions while you are out and about: from a grocery clerk, a gas station attendant, a pedestrian, or a police person. Unless the directions are very simple (as in, "Just around this corner,") repeat the directions and ask any questions that would help clarify for you where you are to go.

★★ Ask a hardware store clerk what she or he would recommend for a stubborn plumbing problem.

★★ Especially if you plan on moving out of your area, call your utility and phone service and ask them to send you a letter of reference regarding your credit record with them.

- ★★ Call a restaurant or store you've never been to and ask for directions.
- ★★ Write a letter to a company that made a product you bought; ask a question, express your concern, or give any feedback you have about the product.
- ★★ Look at the beginning of your phone book for a list of local attractions. Whether or not you're sure you'll visit one, look for one that interests you more than the others, and call to inquire about hours and days open, fees, or directions.
- ★★ Pick a new intersection in a city you want to get to by bus. Call the bus station and ask which bus to take, pick-up times, and drop-off points.
- ★★ Call a few local sources to find out if there is an Incest Survivors Anonymous group, or other pertinent group, where you are.
- ★★ If you are in college and could use some assistance of any kind, ask for an appointment with your advisor or other appropriate staff person.

★★ Call an insurance agent and ask for a quote on renter's, auto, or other insurance.

★★★ If you hear a domestic disturbance in your neighborhood, call the police for assistance.

★★★ If you would like to, attend a support group meeting in your area.

★★★ If your car has been damaged in an accident, consult with the police department to find out what to do, and fill out a report with an officer if necessary.

★★★ If you are having some trouble with your love relationship or your life in general and would like assistance, call a therapist and ask for a referral.

★★★ If you realize you are having trouble with the stresses of being a parent, call up your local Parents Anonymous or Families Anonymous chapter and see what it has to offer you.

★★★ If you or someone you know is in an abusive relationship, call the local Advocates for Battered Women. The person answering your call will not force you to do anything you don't want to do, whether it's reporting someone's behavior, or revealing the names of the people involved. You may find these phone numbers in your yellow pages under Social Service Organizations, Human Services Organizations, or Crisis Intervention, and many of these have access to more complete lists of specific organizations designed to help you.

Asking For Help From Those You Know

Asking for help from friends and other people we know can seem a bit more sticky because we are afraid we might lose them. But our best allies often enjoy helping us out. Put yourself for a moment in their shoes; wouldn't you like a friend to ask you for help so you could share something you know?

- ★ Ask a friend about a product he has in his house, or a professional service he's used, and ask if he'd recommend it.
- ★ If you don't know how, ask someone you know to show you how to check the oil in your car.

- ★ When you go on a trip, ask a friend to housesit for you while you're away.
- ★ Ask a computer-knowledgeable acquaintance a question you have about your own computer.
- ★ Notice a hobby someone has that you'd like to get into. Ask how she got started in it.
- ★ When an appliance breaks down in your home, ask a friend how you might try to fix it.
- ★ When your car starts making a funny new noise, ask a car-wise friend about it.
- ★★ Invite a friend to go along with you to an auction and ask if she'll explain to you how it works.
- ★★ If you've never gone camping, ask someone to give you some pointers.
- ★★ If you like how someone wears her hair or makeup, ask her how she does it.
- ★★ If you're in a confounding situation at work or with some other friends, ask a close friend what he would do in your situation.

- ★★ Ask a friend to teach you how to check your brake fluid, battery water level, windshield washer fluid, and tire pressure.
- ★★ If you are assembling a complex product you just bought, or bringing a heavy item upstairs, ask someone you know to come over and help you out for a bit.
- ★★ Make your birthday wish list known to your friends.
- ★★★ When you're feeling low or confused, call a friend and ask if she will talk to you for a bit.
- ★★★ If you've never gone skiing or backpacking, invite a friend to go with you for a one- or two-day trip as you try it out.
- ★★★ If you have a date with a friend but you realize you are running shorter on time than you anticipated, call him or her to reschedule.
- ★★★ Ask a friend to bring you soup when you're sick.
- ★★★ If you're just learning to drive, ask a good driver to ride with you while you're learning.
- ★★★ Ask a friend to come pick you up when you're stranded.

★★★ When you are ill or leaving on vacation, ask a friend to come and take care of your pets for you.

Before, it seemed easier to control others' responses and our own uncomfortable feelings of shyness by shielding ourselves behind the habit of not asking. But by not asking, we miss receiving an unpredictable smile or warm eye contact. Where we exercise our real power is by allowing ourselves our own soft and human qualities.

I enjoy letting others help me.

6

Gathering Self-Protection

*To love oneself is the beginning of
a lifelong romance.*

Oscar Wilde

Confusion often occurs when we even consider being more assertive. It is not so difficult for people who as children were given the opportunity to say "no." But since saying "no" was not an option for us, we had to use denial to survive. This is not a defense easily dropped and may still operate in our daily lives. Are there times you only look straight ahead, not seeing who or what darkness lays off to the side? Do you "forget" to check the back seat of your car at night before you get in? Do you feel a kind of recklessness about your own safety sometimes? Do you experience a kind of paralysis or apathy when you know you should be doing something different to be safer? Or do you have a desire to tempt fate?

These feelings of confusion, unawareness of our own intentions, and guilt about not doing better are common. Self-protection is a difficult issue to sort through. We were trained in conflicted ways, so we act in conflicted ways.

It is ironic that self-protection itself seems risky to us. This seems backward because it seems it would be scarier to leave ourselves unprotected. For us, though, protection never worked before, so it is not one of the skills we are adept at using. It's one of the ways our abuse twisted our feelings and thoughts.

Self-protection and vulnerability affect us on many different levels. Many survivors do not like twilight because it means darkness is coming. This was often the time many of us were abused, a time when we were most vulnerable. Tranquilizers are the only way some of us can go to sleep. Some of us are routinely insomniac, have looming flashbacks, cannot sleep alone, feel scared lying prone, experience more pain in the evening, cannot sleep well with a new lover, must sleep clothed, or wake up at the smallest sounds. These effects are all part of hypervigilance. A childlike part of us still feels the need to remain on guard.

Naming the Fears

Our first step in self-protection is learning how to take care of these fears. How do we do this? First of all, it is best to try identifying what the specific fears are so that we can answer them with ways we are now able to protect ourselves. For example, are we afraid someone will get into the house? If so, we need to look at each individual window and door to show our child self they are locked. Do we feel nervous sleeping in the bedroom but we wouldn't if we were on the couch? Then it's a good idea to give ourselves that option. Are we afraid of being in the dark? We can try leaving a light on to see if that helps. For every named fear, there is an answer for it.

It is usually more difficult to identify the fears than to come up with additional ways to protect ourselves, but if we need some new ideas on how to increase our sense of safety, here are several: we can post Beware of Dog signs on our doors, ask a friend to stay over if we feel especially unnerved, exercise until we're exhausted, drink chamomile tea to induce drowsiness, or begin practicing our own soothing bedtime rituals. We can sleep with objects around us that give us a feeling of power, whether it's a whistle or shriek alarm on the nightstand or a baseball bat hidden under the bed. We can get out of bed any time we want and go for a drink as a reality check, or we can remain awake for an hour and use that time for our own pleasure.

As we learn how to listen to and attend to that scared, vigilant part of ourselves, we find inevitably that our fear decreases and that relaxation can occur more naturally. Sometimes, as we learn this, we find we are even able to relax in new locations.

In the items listed later in the chapter we will cover some small risks, like locking the car doors at night after you get in, to larger ones, like learning from a self-defense course. The items, however, cannot address an underlying fear many of us have, that of having to recognize and face a potential attacker.

Facing A Common Fear

One of our most damaged responses shows up when someone advances into our territory, as when a drunken stranger in a bar puts his arm around us. Denial kicks in with both feet: "He probably doesn't want to hurt *me*." "I must not understand what he's doing." "This can't be what it looks like." "This can't be happening." By the time any of these thoughts form, it can be too late.

It is vital that we recognize this reflex and begin training it out of ourselves, replacing it with a self-preserving one. Ask a good friend to help you with this exercise to help reinforce a new lesson in your body. The goal is to see how quickly you can respond. Your friend is going to pretend to be somebody threatening you. (Be actors if necessary, to help keep off the smiles that naturally occur.) Have your friend walk toward you from across the room. You are standing still with your arms at your sides, facing the "intruder." Your friend will choose at any moment to raise an arm and continue to advance in a slow but threatening manner. At the second you feel the intruder has come too close, flash your hands up, palms facing outward, and firmly say "No!" just as you would to stop a dog from misbehaving. Your friend stops as soon as you say it.

Your friend can start varying the advance. You can stand partially sideways to the intruder, if you like, to find out when you can see the first motion. See how quick you can be, even crouching with your body to involve more of your muscles.

Exchange roles and try it that way if you want to. Try to name the feelings, like fear at seeing a mean look on the face of your friend, or feeling scared of saying no to your friend. Speak of them and then let them fall to the side as you go forward.

It doesn't really matter that a friend won't likely advance on you like this, or that a simple "no" in real life won't make an attacker disappear. What's important is that we discover our boundaries.

It would be a simple matter if we found one boundary that worked for all situations, but different situations call for different boundaries. Making love means practicing an intimate boundary near the skin level, but during a disagreement it is helpful when our boundaries are firmly outside of us to help us keep our feelings intact, unconfused by someone else's. The truth is that many of us were not allowed to learn about personal boundaries, and if we have a weak one we often carry it too close to ourselves. At that level, someone else's wishes always seem larger than our own. We can't hear the triggers of our feelings, and someone endangering us gets too close before we feel justified in pushing them away. The goal is to nudge your boundaries outward.Make a little room for yourself to think and feel. Here are some gentle ways to help.

Laying Out Our Boundaries
- ★ Practice locking all your doors at night. Use all the locks on each door.
- ★ Sing in the shower. Find your voice, even celebrate it, so that later if you want to use

its power to call your dog or shout for help, your voice won't be a stranger to you.
- ★ Prevent breakdowns. Keep your bike tires and other parts in good shape. Keep up on your car care. Maintain a quarter tank of gas or more at all times.
- ★ Winterize your car if necessary with a snow shovel, jumper cables, and other tools that are effective in your geographic area.
- ★ Practice walking straight, strong, and confident in public places.
- ★ Hang up on an obscene phone call.
- ★ If you are a woman traveling alone for business or vacation, visit your public library and check out the books that address travel situations and tips.
- ★ Take up a sport that will increase your reflexes, like ping pong, or an exercise that will increase your muscle tone, like walking or swimming.
- ★ Practice not telling new acquaintances too much about yourself at first.

★★ If a street or parking area at night looks shadowy or threatening, leave and find another one that's better lit.
★★ When you take your car to an unknown mechanic and you fear being treated unfairly, take an auto-wise friend with you.
★★ Buy a whistle from an athletic store. Bring it with you when you anticipate walking in strange places, or leave one beside your bed.
★★ Take up racquetball or volleyball or another vigorous sport where shouts or grunts are well accepted.
★★ When someone knocks at your door, look through the peephole to see who it is or ask, "Who is it?"
★★ Tell a telephone salesperson you don't want to buy anything.
★★ Join a choral group to strengthen your voice.
★★ Call a local boating supply store and ask if they supply or can order a pocket-size air horn or shriek alarm. This ten- to fifteen-dollar deterrent can be used in the face of a would-be attacker, especially if you don't feel sure you could blow a whistle loudly

enough to attract attention. Keeping one beside your bed may also increase your feeling of security.

★★★ Tell a door-to-door salesperson that you are not interested, and follow through by closing the door.

★★★ When someone on the street comes at you drunkenly or asking for money, walk quickly away if he or she gets too close.

★★★ If you are a woman, see if your local Rape Crisis Center offers a short course on self-protection techniques specifically for women. Enroll in a class.

★★★ Read your poetry at an open-mike reading, in front of friends, to find out the strength of your voice.

★★★ If you are ready for a longer-term commitment, enroll in Aikido, karate, or a similar discipline. Re-enroll in advanced courses so that you become proficient in fending off an aggressive person.

★★★ Take a friend to a deserted railroad track and see how far down the track you can hear either of you yell. Or go to a busy train track or a bustling airport runway and when one of these vehicles roars by, see if you can hear your own shouts over the noise.

When we practice the right to protect ourselves, we react less with the old rigidity of fear. We become keen in our perception of the moment, which is vital to our success.

Each day has the potential of being a little brighter than the last one. By learning self-preservation, we reclaim our birthright of protecting all that is dear to us.

The more I maintain healthy boundaries, the stronger I feel.

7

Asserting Consumer Rights

The main thing in life is not to be afraid to be human.

Pablo Casals

What Are Our Rights?

Figuring out our consumer rights can be mystifying. It involves again that word "protection," as in "consumer protection." Because we were unprotected as youngsters and had no sheltering role models, we may wonder how we can protect ourselves as adults when it comes to the products we buy and the services we use. We may have a complaint but feel discouraged about having to face a number of strangers who seem to be in authority.

For example, nowadays bowls, tea balls, and blenders come packed and taped tightly into boxes filled with stuffing. You usually don't know until you get home if it's the color advertised on the box, if it was broken in shipping, it has all the pieces enclosed, including instructions and warranties. You don't know the name of the inventor, much less the name of the machines used to make it, or what exactly caused a defect in your product. We cannot always repair these complex products we buy, especially if they have computerized parts that break down. We feel intimidated by the next step. We don't know who to consult or who to trust. We risk feeling visible if we complain. We dread facing that anonymous business crowd of people in the sky. Besides all this, we have to get beyond feeling "to blame," as if we will be confronted with breaking the object in the first place.

Nonetheless, only one person at a time can talk with us on the telephone, as only one person can read a letter from us. Our consumer rights are as simple as this: we deserve to get what we understand we are paying for. And if we got what was promised and the service is still not quite what we hoped for, we have the right to go to someone new the next time.

While this may sound deceptively simple, the task becomes complicated when our complaints concern the service of a person we are familiar with. This involves services like lawn-mowing, dry cleaning, hair styling, massage, and therapy. Because we may not want to doubt a person's intentions, we hesitate to bring up a wish we have for how a service could be done more to our liking. We rationalize that we can live with it the way it is. Especially where education, licenses, and degrees are involved, we tend to bow to others who claim expertise.

A good example is when patients talk about how they are treated by their doctors. Some patients sit for a long time in a waiting room, and even when their time with the doctor is rushed and they feel brushed off, they don't confront the doctor or the staff about it. This may occur repeatedly. A complicating factor for incest survivors is that it can take us weeks or months to make an appointment with a doctor who is going to see us partially naked, or touch our bodies. We may stick with a doctor rather than face the uncertain search process again.

It always seems easier to stay with a professional we've had for a long time, but no matter who it is, we deserve to feel good about services we pay for. Ideally, the whole point of service-exchanging is that each party ends up winning.

Whenever anyone treats us with less attention or respect than we feel we deserve and we continue to submit to it, it costs us. It represses our level of self-esteem, it keeps us linked to a limited past, and most importantly, it allows no room for new self-respect to grow. Each step we make to take what is rightfully ours increases our self-esteem, which makes each succeeding step easier.

Our Own Consumer Protection

In order to make progress on this issue, we don't need to suddenly erupt in front of someone, or launch into a full-blown confrontation. We can simply begin by asking a question of a professional, by shaking our heads and saying, "No, I don't understand," or by asking for another explanation. We can take other steps that will serve us better in the long run. This might include writing a letter to our doctor or to his or her office manager. Or, in the case of products, we could start a file for receipts on larger items we might return if they're not to our preference or they malfunction within the warranty period. Here are some more ways:

- ★ Look for sewing mistakes and missing buttons on clothing before buying. Try out the zipper.
- ★ Open an egg carton before buying to make sure no eggs are cracked.
- ★ Use the telephone to do some price comparison shopping on a large item like a washer or a sofa.
- ★ When you have any questions about your rights, look for a telephone number in your phone book for Consumer Protection.
- ★ When you go to a new hairdresser or a new veterinarian and you're not quite satisfied, don't return. Find a new one.
- ★★ While in line, check your sales receipt for accuracy if you think it looks incorrect.
- ★★ When a part on your car is recalled, take it in for replacement.

- ★★ Write a letter to a company expressing your dissatisfaction with either a product of theirs or the treatment you received from one of their clerks.
- ★★ Write a letter to a television network if you are particularly disturbed about a show.
- ★★ Return a product you just bought that doesn't work like it should, or get a credit for a food item you opened that was spoiled.
- ★★ Ask a professional whose services you use a question about something you don't understand. Or ask her a question about where she went to school, or how she likes her business.
- ★★★ If you feel unusually sore after a chiropractic adjustment, mention it to your chiropractor on your next appointment; or if your masseur skips or skims over one of your sore muscle areas, ask him to give it more attention.

- ★★★ If you buy an appliance that works fine, but then you read a health warning about it in a newspaper, return it.
- ★★★ When you feel hurried in your visit with your doctor, ask her or him to schedule a little more time for your next appointment so you can go over some questions you have. Then, before the next appointment, write down the questions you would like to have answered.
- ★★★ Even if you've been with a doctor or dentist for years, look for a new one if you're dissatisfied. The phone book or a friend's referral are two ways to begin. Another is to look in the yellow pages under Dentist or Doctor Information and Referral Services for help in locating a professional compatible with your needs.
- ★★★ Consider filing a complaint against any therapist or clergyperson who sexually or otherwise abused you.

If you wanted to start and run a good business, you would want feedback from your customers. It would be both rewarding and challenging, but it would support your goal to make as many people as possible happy with your service. When you have feedback about a product, offer it to the company who made it. Let them share your satisfaction, or give them a chance to regain your trust.

I deserve to get my money's worth.

8

Being Seen

It is the nature of friendship not to be hidden.

St. Thomas Aquinas

When we break visibility into its parts, we find two main ways we make ourselves known to others: by having our bodies represent who we are (physical visibility), and by speaking about our private feelings (emotional visibility). Our level of emotional visibility is more easily detectable in our friendly and intimate relationships, which we will cover in Chapter Ten on Assertiveness in Relationships.

Physical Visibility

Visibility before strangers is a tad simpler because we are less emotionally tied to people we don't know. But while physical visibility before strangers may be a lesser risk to take, it can still be a frightening prospect.

This supersensitivity about our vulnerability began, of course, when we were children being violated by hitting hands, or invaded by someone bigger than we were. We were not allowed to luxuriate in a fullness of ourselves; instead we were intimidated into being quiet, forced to find ways to fit in, made to "disappear." We even consciously wished we could hide, and the sad fact is many of us wished to be dead.

The notion of living a vibrant lifestyle is a farfetched idea for many abuse survivors. Since we felt too large or too exposed when we lived in a child-sized body, it is easy to understand why we often need to hide inside our adult-sized bodies. We may do things like drink too much to numb ourselves, eat too little to attain that desired smaller size, or eat too much to desensitize ourselves or build a buffer of weight to hide behind.

Many of the issues specific to incest survivors involve some kind of visibility. If we felt shamed enough, we associate being visible with being under the spotlight of others' judging eyes. And even if we weren't overtly criticized, we found out that by just *being* in our life, by merely appearing in our physical form, harm came to us. There is a certain way we are like the trembling dog we see from time to time that crawls up to us on its belly. It looks like it has been beaten many times before, and chances are it has. It learned from those experiences that its environment was hostile. To adapt, the dog adopted this cowering behavior because it was rewarded by not being hit as often or as hard, by showing itself to be inferior in the pecking order. Making itself smaller has been its adaptation; it continues to anticipate cruelty from strangers even quite a long time later in its life.

We speak kindly to an intimidated animal to bring it forward. We too can be coaxed forward with gentle words. We do some of this for ourselves, by showing ourselves new ways with careful risk-taking, and by choosing friends and lovers who can show us with their words and deeds that they are trustworthy and supportive of our growth.

Taking the Stage

The exciting aspect to visibility is that it can provide the delightful experience of feeling recognized. One of the ways to visualize this is to think of something you make or write, whether it's poetry, journal entries, art, music, or a craft. Imagine some of your work being performed on a stage by others or yourself, or presented at an exhibit. Now imagine that a couple of people in the audience want to meet the creator to express their excitement about what you do. Maybe they enjoy the colors or sounds you put together and want to compliment you on your creativity. Perhaps they see a theme running through your work that you never noticed before. The effect of their attention is nurturing for you. You feel fed, even "pumped up." This need for recognition is as old as we are.

Think for a moment about the very visible work some people do, like what we see televised: rock groups and their back-up dancers, pitchers and other players on a baseball team, free throw shooters in a basketball game, paired opponents in tennis, jockeys, child actors in commercials, and all the hundreds of actors and comic performers that are the backbone of programs. None of these people got where they are without walking through their fear of visibility. On the contrary: they've come to love being visible!

Of course, you may not want to be a world-famous opera singer or a politician, but on the other hand, we are all visible to others in our own ways. We dress a certain way. We walk a particular way in public. We ask the waiter to take our order. And then, sometimes we're not so visible, like when the waiter doesn't hear our quiet voice and we have to ask again. Or when we sometimes wear clothes to hide a part of our bodies we're not happy with.

If we walk down the street with averted eyes and hunched shoulders, we're not telling the world anything new. There's something to be said for dressing ourselves in an air of confidence—our breathing changes, we notice things we didn't notice before, and people are less likely to avert their eyes when passing us. Self-esteem grows like an upward spiral; with a little generation, the rewards that come will circle back to reinforce more self-esteem. It even causes us to make decisions differently, which includes sound judgment on protecting ourselves, and healthy risk-taking.

One of the things that may prevent us from feeling our attractiveness is the fear we have of attracting people we don't want. It's unfortunate that this occurs, that we sometimes have to ignore the attentions of someone we are not interested in or come up with some communication that makes the person leave us alone. But if you are still worried, have a little faith in yourself that when those situations arise, you will deal with them the best way you know how. Remember that as you exercise that skill, too, you'll get better at it, and your worry will diminish. You'll be able to walk about with a greater sense of freedom, just as you want to.

Critical Parent, Take a Break!

The next time you're out in public, entertain the idea that strangers' main goal in life is not to converge on you and mentally criticize you. Strangers are not our parents. They don't have so much time that they can also focus on every stranger around them. They may be thinking about their laundry, or an errand they have to do today, or any other idea that takes up brain activity. Another creative way to think about this is to remember that one out of every several persons you see is also an incest survivor. They too, may be struggling with the thought that you as a stranger are judging *them*.

Body image is another stumbling block for many of us, and a whole book could more adequately address the ways we've long felt convinced we don't look 'good enough.' We may look at ourselves with the harshness of people in our past, seeing thick ankles or unmentionable hair. Instead of typecasting strangers into judgmental parent figures, practice acknowledging the uncertainty that we cannot be sure that strangers are thinking a particular negative thought about us.

We can practice this new realization while trying any of the following ideas.

Taking Our Place in the World

- ★ Stop at a water fountain and lean over to take a drink.
- ★ Go to a change-making machine with a dollar bill and make change.
- ★ Walk with a spring in your step on a city street.
- ★ Take a bit more time at the gas station—wash every one of your windows, for example.
- ★ Go to a new or used car lot when it's closed and look at the cars on display.
- ★ Spend an hour in your house alone, dressed in your swim suit.
- ★ Buy a bit of new makeup and try wearing it a little differently.
- ★ When someone compliments you on how you look, try not to diminish it or become "foggy" emotionally. Let the comment soak in, and practice saying a gracious "Thank you."
- ★ Pick a day to bike or bus to work instead of driving your car.

- ★ At a new video store where you aren't a member, fill out an application to become one.
- ★★ Go to a food vending machine and buy an item when you're hungry and without better options.
- ★★ Enroll in a summer mini-course at a college.
- ★★ When you walk down the street, look at your reflection in windows.
- ★★ After your gas tank is filled and your bill is paid, take up a little more time by lifting the hood and checking your oil.
- ★★ Take a camera to a downtown street and take some pictures.
- ★★ Go to a new automatic teller machine and use it.
- ★★ With the idea of going for a bike ride or a walk, pick a part of your body you're not especially fond of, like your wrists or calves, and wear clothing that lets this part get some fresh air too. Enjoy yourself as you get your exercise.

- ★★ Go to a ritzier clothing or lingerie store than you're used to, and if the sales clerk asks, say you're just looking.
- ★★ Let someone take a picture with you included. Try not to hide behind someone or something.
- ★★ Take the developed photo from the item above, put it into an album, and leave it in your living room.
- ★★★ Take up a new sport.
- ★★★ Go to a car lot when it's open and tell any salesperson who asks that you're just looking.
- ★★★ With others present, look into the mirror of a public restroom and straighten your hair or clothing.
- ★★★ Put on your swimsuit and go to a public beach and go swimming. (If you don't like your suit, go to a department store and try some on.)
- ★★★ Have a friend take a bunch of pictures of you. From those, pick one that you like better than the others and post it in your house somewhere.

★★★ If you happen to witness an auto accident or a crime of some kind, wait long enough for the police to arrive to give your account.

★★★ Have a picture of you reprinted to send inside holiday cards.

When we practice listening to our internal voices and practice being seen by others, we take the opportunity to start new trends with ourselves. Practice taking up space, and taking up time. Grow into yourself, and become yourself as much as you possibly can.

I see myself through other's eyes and I like what I see.

9

Living in the Body

*The heart has its reasons,
which reason cannot know.*

Pascal

When the Body Seemed Like Our Enemy

For an incest survivor, simply living within the body as an adult can be a monumental challenge. What do we mean by "living in the body?" Don't we always live in it?

When a child feels tortured, there is no sane reason to stay present to feel the pain. When an adult forces a child to do things with her body she doesn't want to do, gives her several reasons to cry, and then threatens her if she dares make a sound, the child literally cannot stay within the body to feel everything. The marvel of this is that each of us independently found the creativity to make this dissociation happen. We survived by using it.

What happens when we dissociate as adults? It begins when we perceive a threat. Whether or not the danger is really there anymore, the point is that we perceive it that way. When our response is triggered, it may be characterized by repeated and rapid anxious feelings and thoughts, and the mind begins to "elevate" away from the body. In fact, the physical consequences of this mind-body split show up in our headaches, sore throats, tight jaws, and stiff and aching necks.

When we split, we may be thinking about anything except what is at hand. Composing a letter in our minds suddenly becomes more important than feeling the hands of our lover on us. Or we go numb. We feel foggy; no words come to us, but we know we're not quite feeling our partner kissing us.

Splitting, while most common during lovemaking, occurs on many more subtle levels as well. It happens when we are doing other physical things, like taking a bath. How much do we really enjoy the dripping of water on our skin or the silky smoothness of soap? When we walk upstairs, do we feel any of our leg muscles doing the work? Do we walk somewhat stiffly? When we're sitting in a chair, is it an effort to call up the energy needed to go get something? Do we feel the crinkliness of dish-suds when we wash dishes? When we make popcorn, do we smell the first aroma from the pan?

Since the body is the medium through which we experience all physical life, our abuse can affect us in countless day-to-day activities. But as the examples are limitless, so now are the opportunities. The question is, would you like to feel more of that playful child living within you?

Making Friends With Our Body

As children, we did not have enough safe physical feeling to find much joy in it. The truth is, it can be joyful, but only when we feel secure. Thus, to find our way in this journey, it is vital to discover ways to encourage our feeling of safety in the world.

One way to do this is to promise yourself that you won't do all of the exercises that follow unless you feel safe in each step. A characteristic of incest survivors is our "all-or-nothing" way of thinking, where we are unforgiving of ourselves unless we complete every single goal no matter how unrealistic it might be. In the following exercise, you may feel a bit anxious after doing one or two of the parts; regard this sign as an ally, and recognize it as valuable. Rest for as long as you want. Another way to feel safer is to commit only to reading the parts but not doing them until later, when you're ready. Approach this territory with a sense of fun, because that is the goal, to find new ways to enjoy your body.

This is a sense check:

Sight. Look at, and soak in, the colors and textures while facing one direction.

Smell. Breathe a full breath of the air: does it smell like anything right now?

Taste. Do you taste anything? Does your tongue feel your teeth?

Sound. Close your eyes for ten to twenty seconds. Count how many different sounds are in your environment at this moment.

Touch. Starting at the top of your body, carefully count the places you feel something touching you, as in pressure from a chair while sitting, or the weight of clothes, or an air draft on your skin.

Internal touch. Take a quiet moment to see if you can feel your heart beating; you may also be able to feel another pulse beating somewhere in your body.

Breathing. Take one big, slow breath, as if you are going to yawn, filling up from your diaphragm below your ribs, and gradually sending air in to the middle and upper parts of your lungs. Can you feel the movements of your ribs? This last step is a good exercise to do any time since we tend to be shallow breathers. More breath brings more sensitivity, more awareness.

Of course, the main reason we try not to have too much body awareness is because we're afraid of feelings and discomfort that may arise. We were victimized while feeling pain before, so now it is difficult not to feel victimized by pain itself. Some of us ignore pain no matter what the cost. We hope the irritation will go away with the same kind of denial we used to wish the incest would disappear on its own. Some of us are prime candidates for hypochondria. We find more value or self-worth while in crisis or pain than in feeling inconspicuously healthy. And many incest survivors have "floating" pain that may disappear from one part of the body after treatment but will almost simultaneously reappear in another part of the body. It is as if a wound from the incest is crying for recognition.

Pain, however, need not be viewed as a perpetrator but as an aid, just as feelings can be. Pain tells us when we don't feel good, and when we learn to listen to it, it tells us its wisdom. This relearning process takes time, patience, and a willingness to modify how we usually react to it. With practice we become more pain-free because we start listening to our bodies sooner, preventing the need for a red flag to catch our attention.

If uncomfortable feelings arise while doing any of the items that follow, use your breath as a lifeboat. Without hyperventilating, ride the breath as smoothly as you can. Consider that your breath can be less labored, more free, and even effortless. Ride this boat and then you can dip into the feeling as you feel ready.

Moving Into the Body

- ★ Burn incense or a candle in your room.
- ★ Listen to wind chimes, a recording of bird sounds, or a favorite piece of music.
- ★ Ask yourself if your room temperature is perfectly comfortable for you, and if not, adjust it until it is.
- ★ In the morning take a drink of cool water just to feel it falling down the inside of your "pipes."
- ★ When you prepare to go outside, dress appropriately so you won't be uncomfortably cold or hot. Take a few extra clothes if you think the weather might change.
- ★ Remember to smell dinner as you make it. If you can't detect the smell, walk out of the house and come back in to the aroma.

- ★ While driving, look in the rearview mirror periodically to see if your face looks relaxed.
- ★ Pay attention to small irritations like chapped lips or a hangnail, and tend to them.
- ★ Take a bath instead of a shower.
- ★ When you are sitting down to eat, whether alone or with your family, first pick your favorite dish and utensils. Then eat your food with pleasure, taking more time than usual to feel the tastes and textures. Recognize when you feel sated.
- ★★ Instead of photographing your way through a vacation, leave your camera behind for a few days.
- ★★ Acknowledge those parts of your body you don't feel a kinship with. Start with one of them. Let it tell you what it needs to say. If you feel ready, touch it so it knows it's alive. Buy it a gift.
- ★★ Practice good listening skills with your friends.

- ★★ Shop at a health food co-op for new foods your body enjoys.
- ★★ While in private, spend an hour in your house while in the nude.
- ★★ Assign a full-length mirror in your bedroom or bathroom to be your friend. Look into it periodically, moving your body as you do it. This will help shift your static notions of what you look like.
- ★★★ Go to a quiet weight room and lift weights to strengthen yourself. If you haven't been coached on how to do it properly, be sure to ask a friend or instructor.
- ★★★ When you go to a party, talk as much as anybody else. Be involved as much as you can, leaving the "observer" role to someone else.
- ★★★ Join a health club and use your membership to swim or play in a sport with others.
- ★★★ Call for an appointment to have a massage.
- ★★★ Consult a holistic health care doctor about a pain you've had, whether it's severe or chronic.

★★★ While feeling safe at home, take off your glasses or remove your contacts to feel your connections with the ground a little more. Identify any feelings of anxiety that arise.

★★★ Practice finding out what your body really craves: a rest, a hug, more physical work, sunshine, a little sexual play, or a certain food. Try giving it what it's asking for.

We can afford to listen to our bodies again. We can ensure that it is safe to do so; it even becomes exciting and enjoyable to discover it again.

My body helps me learn about myself.

10

Assertiveness in Relationships

The meeting of two personalities is like the contact of two chemical substances: if there is any reaction, both are transformed.

C.G. Jung

Emotional Visibility

The word "visibility" is making another appearance here, as in "emotional visibility." Who needs any more of it? Aren't we as visible as we want to be in our relationships?

To get a picture of how balanced our love relationship or friendships are, picture how much respect or weight you tend to give your spouse or friend. When she or he asks you to do something, do you do it without stopping to ask yourself if you really want to? When your parents invite you to their house, do you go even though you're not sure why? When your partner wants to make love, do you feel obliged to acquiesce?

If you picture the "garden of respect" you give to others, it is no doubt a lively place full of large plants flowering, full of energy. In the garden you afford to yourself, are the plant leaves wilted a bit from not enough watering? Have a few branches turned brown? Are there only a few butterflies and birds playing above it?

When we build our self-esteem, it doesn't mean we need to cut down our respect for others. It only means we are going to build ours up to equal status. We deserve that much. This means we spend more time tending to our own rebuilding. At times we will leave our friends free to do their own nurturing. We respect them enough to afford them the dignity to find their own way when they need to.

Actually, assertiveness in relationships is connected to the liveliness and energy expressed between two people. When communication breaks down and both people become complacent about it, the relationship eventually loses its "zing."

In the beginning of any relationship, we have some excitement about getting to know the other person. As long as we keep making ourselves known, asserting who we are, and listening to each other, ours is a rich friendship. Within a love relationship that seems lackluster, chances are we aren't taking enough risks by being more visible. But what should we talk about?

Improving Communications

This is where we can reap the value of disagreements. Our discomforts or irritations are a fine place to begin, but how do we start? While clear communication contains a few simple concepts, these become muddied if we cannot disentangle ourselves from laying blame or projections, or being convinced that the other doesn't regard us as highly as we'd like. To reverse some of the damages to our trust, we need to respect our lover's words and actions. In what way has our partner been trying lately to convince us that we matter to her or him? Did we listen very carefully? Are we more attached to our old suspicions than to hearing that we're really loved by this person?

Keen listening, then, is one of the starting points for effective communication. Another is the decision to own our own feelings. What this means is that we won't be blaming anyone else for "causing" a feeling in us. Instead of, "You're making me angry," or "You hurt me when you said that," it becomes, "I feel angry when you do that," and "I feel hurt about something you said earlier." The difference is subtle but important.

If you want to try it, the sentence that follows can be, "What I'm hearing is that you think I'm _____ (demanding, insensitive, arrogant, emotional, unattractive, ignorant, stubborn, etc.)." When we discover what we think we are hearing, it often turns out to be something we heard from our parents. We often project onto our partner our sensitivity to feeling hurt. However, what we interpreted may not be at all what our partner was trying to convey.

The dramatic effect of this exercise comes when our partner listens to us, reclarifies what he or she meant, and we release the old belief long enough to hear what our partner is trying to say. This is where real change occurs and trust is rebuilt. After uncovering the roots of these feelings and dealing with them honestly, a couple invariably experiences relief and closeness.

Of course, it is possible that our partner was distracted at the time and made an insensitive comment. An apology is another appropriate option. And it is up to us to trust that our partner's intentions were not malicious.

This doesn't mean that if we are with an unkind or abusive partner we should naively believe everything he or she tells us. If, for example, you are riding out your child self's hope that your partner will change, chances are you are manufacturing evidence that your partner loves you more than he or she does. If you are beginning to question your partner's true intentions, screen out the words for a while and pay close and strict attention to what he or she does. Words can be custom-made to include excuses, untruths, denial and false promises, but actions always tell the real story.

Guessing vs. Sharing

Let's take a look at an example of communication that is complex for us—asserting ourselves when it comes to sex. The first scenario shows a lack of effective communication, the second a more positive interaction.

The first couple's ritual has been to make love on Saturday night after the kids are in bed. As Saturday evening approaches, the woman is in the other rooms of the house, doing things that "need doing" and checking on the children. When he comes up to her, she doesn't look at him, and makes her way out of the room to do the next task. She may slip out of his hug or appear agitated but neither of them say anything about it. The most damaging effects are what they imagine and walk away with: he feels perplexed, disappointed, and maybe resentful; and she feels perhaps like a sex object, or that he's more sex-driven than she.

The other couple's ritual is the same. This woman notices she wants to avoid sex, and decides to try to talk about it.

She says, "I'm scared to talk about this—do you have a minute?"

He says, "Sure," and puts his book down.

She sits down and says, "I don't know what's bothering me, but it's about lovemaking tonight. I don't even want to tell you this, but I don't feel like it tonight."

"Okay, let's talk about it. I'd rather talk with you than have you feel bad about something."

These two people can really find out about each other. They are casting off the projections and ideas they held about each other. They have begun to uncover their real needs and desires.

Sometimes when we own a feeling, voice it, and perhaps even say how someone can help us out, our listener may become upset. To keep yourself from feeling muddled by someone else's issues, you can listen to him or her, but hold your own feeling in a special place. Let nothing attack it, let nothing confuse you. Your feeling remains true and real, no matter what.

Always remember that when you need some outside support as you make these changes, you can meet with a friend or consult with a therapist.

Showing the Inner Self
- ★ Two of you are traveling and you are lost. Your companion thinks you should go one way but you disagree and speak up.
- ★ While you are in a store, your toddler begins screaming for a certain object or wanting a specific kind of food. You simply say no.
- ★ Your kids and your spouse have been contributing to the general disarray around the house. Express your feeling about it and request their help in picking up after themselves more often.
- ★ The baby is crying and you've been doing most of the child care. Ask your partner to take care of the baby.
- ★ As a single parent, you are worn out after not having a night off in weeks. Figure out a way to get a sitter to give you some hours off.

- ★ You realize you want some alone time with your partner and suggest making a date to get together.
- ★ Your partner wants to paint a room or buy a car or make any other change in your mutual lives. Make your opinions known.
- ★ You're taking a long car ride with others and you find you're getting stiff or hungry. You make a request to stop at a rest area soon.
- ★★ Your mother or friends are coming over to your house. Leave one room in your house as untidy as it is usually.
- ★★ Your child arrives home from high school and wants to talk with you about something and you're so tired you know you won't be a good listener. Ask if it can wait, and if so, make a plan for after you've taken a nap.
- ★★ Ask your partner to read parts of a book on incest or find a section for partners she or he can read.
- ★★ If a parent or spouse wants you to cut your hair, change your job, or lose weight, decide for yourself what you want to do.
- ★★ Call up a friend when you're feeling low.

- ★★ With your partner, set aside a few moments each night in bed for each of you to speak of unresolved feelings from the day.
- ★★ If your partner asks you to go somewhere you've been before and didn't enjoy yourself, simply decline.
- ★★★ Ask your therapist for something you need.
- ★★★ Ask your partner to stay awake with you for a few moments of closeness after sex.
- ★★★ If a friend invites you to get together and you'd rather not, decline for now. Reaffirm that you'll call later.
- ★★★ Say no to sex for right now, or even talk with your partner about being celibate for a specified number of weeks to help your feeling of safety. Make regular plans to talk about what both of you are feeling.
- ★★★ Confront a friend or your lover with something you feel hurt or angry about.
- ★★★ If you've tested negative for HIV antibodies and want your new partner to be tested before you engage in sexual play, ask your partner to have a blood test.

★★★ If something feels unresolved during one of your therapy sessions, or if you feel too scared to express your anger or hurt, tell your therapist you feel uncertain about bringing these things up.

★★★ If you feel your relationship is not as successful as it could be, and you feel that anger is going unresolved, suggest to your partner the idea of finding a couples therapist to help.

It always seems as though it might be easier to start over with fresh friendships than it is to do the work of changing the old ones. But we would still not have developed the skill of making ourselves visible. Continue to breathe life into your wants and needs as well; they are just as important as those of the people closest to you.

I have the right to express my honest feelings to my intimate friends.

11

Sex and Intimacy

Love must be learned and learned again and again; there is no end to it.

Katherine Anne Porter

Untangling Our Confusion

Sex is one of the most confounding issues for an incest survivor. We met sex for the first time under threat of punishment or death. Sex became the antithesis of fun and freedom. Having a body meant we were potentially a target at any time. Sex, or the possibility of it, came to mean worry, repulsion, dissociation, and fear. Indeed, many of us still lose our voices when even a hint of sex is in the air.

When we were repressed, so was our sexuality. As other parts of our personality became bound up—our rage, our tears, our other powers—our sexuality became bound up too.

The good news is that it is helpful to work on sexual issues, but it is not always necessary. As you free up other feelings of betrayal and sadness and fear, it will help relax your sexual anxieties as well.

Because there is so much hurt surrounding this issue, there is much to re-learn, but this needn't prompt us to overwhelm ourselves with risk-taking. For example, it's not a gentle goal to suddenly commit to telling our lover every single private and shameful thought we have about sex. For if we force ourselves to do something we're not ready for, we risk re-traumatizing the child in us by betraying ourselves.

We should address some underlying questions we may have about betrayal. Suppose we're not sure we want to make love but our partner would like to. When we say yes, are we betraying ourselves? What if this happens quite a lot?

First of all, many of us struggle with these kinds of questions. This feeling we have of being unable to know ourselves or what we want is strongly characteristic of survivors. In fact, until we find other ways, it is our norm to give ourselves away. Our goal need not be too drastic, but we can decide to listen to ourselves more and give ourselves away less. It is important to find compassion for ourselves about these difficult situations. Eventually, with practice, we will find we are making love only when we feel safe, and we will be happy doing it. Until that occurs for us, it is helpful to continue identifying our negative associations about sex. (For more clarification about particular sexual thoughts and feelings we have as survivors of incest, refer to Appendix C, "Am I the Only One?" and Appendix D, "What *Do* I Feel During Sex?")

While we're at it, let's clear up a few other ideas about sex. First of all, babies and children are not inherently sexual. They do not have a sex drive that makes them seduce adults. If we see anything sexual in a child, this is the projection of our adult viewpoint. It has nothing to do with what the child is experiencing. Since using the word "sensual" might be unclear, we can look at the youngster as a "sense" creature. Children explore the world using their mouths, by listening to mommy's voice, and through touch.

Play and Sex

Even now that we are adults, it is still our child self that enjoys the play of touch. In fact, during involved lovemaking, our child self is thoroughly engaged in having a good time too. Learning how to listen to this child is the secret behind knowing whether to proceed to lovemaking or not. For example, if she is panicky that sex is going to be used against her, and we plunge ahead anyway, part of us will need to vacate the body. And when we acknowledge how uncertain we feel about lovemaking, and even voice one of those ashamed or unpleasant feelings to our partner, it strengthens the bond between us and our child self. It also gives our partner the chance to support us for being honest, and to clarify what her or his wishes are and to help us identify a mistaken belief we had.

Naming some of these shadowy, ashamed feelings is half the battle. Remember that identifying these feelings does not bind you to any next step. You are not obliged to expose everything to your lover. If you want, you can ask her or him to read parts of this book. Or you can wait until you're ready to verbalize certain feelings or questions. Your partner may turn out to be more supportive than you anticipated!

Also, it is important for your lover to realize that she or he has special concerns as the partner to an incest survivor. It is recommended that he or she read a chapter for partners out of any helpful book on incest.

This is not to say that you are "the problem" in the relationship, even if you believe you are. The truth is, no matter how hard you try, you cannot monopolize the box of Problems and Issues in a relationship. Nobody is immune from the personal issues he or she needs to work on, including your partner. Have you ever considered that your partner was attracted to you (consciously or not) in part because you are an incest survivor? Attractions are not random. Chances are high that your partner has issues to work out from his or her past that resonate in some way with yours.

New Intimacies

Sometimes love partners are convinced that sex is the only way to be intimate. If you decide a sabbatical from sex would help you, the distinct advantage is that both of you will be challenged to be a little more creative about how to meet your intimacy needs. You might find that you both enjoy cuddling on the couch in front of a movie, hiking in the woods on a weekend, or reading poetry to each other.

Here is an exercise you might try. Select two pieces of blank paper and a pencil. Then, sit for a moment inside your child self, the one who was hurt by other people. Through this child's eyes, take a look at your adult-sized body in the nude, let's say in a standing position. How does this child see it? Perhaps certain parts look distorted to him or her. Perhaps the whole body looks a certain size. Now put your pencil in your non-dominant hand and draw whatever comes to you. However it comes out is fine—you are not looking for a resemblance to your body, you are reproducing your child's feelings about your body.

When you are finished with this body picture, take a long and gentle look at what you drew. Invite your child self to come and sit beside you. You are going to draw a new picture for him or her on the second sheet of paper. Visualize for a moment while in your adult frame of mind *how you would like to feel* about yourself, and then, using your dominant hand, make a sketch of your body once more. Again, accuracy is not needed. The game is just to enjoy your lines as you make them.

When you are finished, let your child absorb a little of your last picture. Bring this little bit of light to her or his long-held view, blowing a little breath of hope into the new way of living that you picture for both of you.

Intimate Play

Any of the following ideas can help us strengthen our affinity for intimacy and its expression. Please note that the first level of risk listed is to be done with the understanding that none of it turns into sexual play:

- ★ Sit down with your partner and some paper. Then write down ten to twenty things each (other than lovemaking) that would feel like intimate activities to do together. Review both lists and talk about them. If you like, make a plan to do one soon.
- ★ Ask your partner to give a non-sexual massage to an area of your body you select. Another night, do the same for your partner.
- ★ Thank your partner for something he or she did.
- ★ Take a bath together.
- ★ Find or make a piece of art with pleasing lines and full texture. Display it in your house.
- ★★ Write a journal piece: "How I Feel About Sex is . . .," and "How I Want to Feel About Sex is . . ."
- ★★ Tell your partner something you love about her or his body.
- ★★ Pick a part of your body you're not fond

of, and ask your partner to tell it a few kind and loving things.

★★ Perhaps as a general goal you would like to be more present during sex. Tell your spouse that you would like to take a few moments to explore and express your feelings before proceeding with lovemaking the next few times. Ask how he or she feels about that.

★★ Go out to dinner with your partner dressed in something that makes you feel sexy.

★★ If you realize you feel frightened by the sight of your nude lover walking around the house, talk about it with him or her. Mention, if necessary, that your feeling may not be a permanent one but that you feel a need to tend to it. Talk about options that would work for both of you.

★★ Find a book on erotica at the library and bring it home.

- ★★ Consider being celibate for a while if it would help you feel safer or help to clarify some things for you. Discuss it with your partner.
- ★★★ Tell your lover a sexual fantasy you have. Ask if he or she will tell you one in return.
- ★★★ Visit a lingerie store with your partner. Pick out something fun for one or both of you to wear.
- ★★★ See if you can find a quality erotic film to rent and watch at home.
- ★★★ Order a sex toy for fun.
- ★★★ Take some private time to come up with an idea that arouses you which you could write into a piece of erotica. You could write a fantasy you often have; make it a turn-on for you. Do it knowing you're not going to show it to anybody.
- ★★★ Consider a therapist's help to aid you with your intimacy issues. This might be couples' help, or counseling you choose for yourself.

★★★ Act out a safe sexual fantasy with your partner.

Relationships invariably break down under the strain of secrets kept and projections refueled. Intimacy is borne of openness and the rewards of taking risks with another person. We are never too old to delight in a refreshed feeling of intimacy with our partner.

Sex and talking about sex are safe for me to do with my partner.

12

Assertiveness at Work

Paint as you like and die happy.

Henry Miller

While work is usually associated with structure and responsibility, its opposite, play, is characterized by a carefree, creative attitude. Play means a complete and fulfilling involvement in the moment. Wouldn't it be great if more of the qualities of play went into our work?

When we find satisfaction in the day-to-day work we do, whether it is at an office or at home doing child care or other projects, the whole of our lives feels less strained, more fulfilled, and more rounded. Transition between work and play becomes smoother and less noticeable. We come to find we don't mind so much that Monday morning has arrived, and we don't dread the first day of work after a good vacation.

Our Challenges

Incidentally, most incest survivors have their work cut out for them before they ever take their first job. Our sunken level of self-esteem has stuck to us like a shadow. It is insidious. It keeps some of us from trying college; it keeps others from applying for grants and scholarships; others feel ashamed to ask all the questions we have in class. If we don't earn a degree, we end up in lower-paying jobs. And if we do, we find it difficult to know what treatment we deserve, what pay we should be receiving.

This kind of self-image also keeps us from sending in applications to new employers whose authority we fear, or whose requirements seem outside our abilities, even if they aren't. If we haven't felt valuable in work we have done before, the language of our resume reflects that. Even the print quality, spelling, and punctuation of our resume indicate how we feel about ourselves. Then, when we are called in for an interview, we feel awkward as we try to answer questions about ourselves and make inquiries about the company without appearing as ignorant as we feel. Some make it through all these steps, are offered a job, and then refuse because they still feel sure they will not be able to perform it adequately.

Consequently, we may retain a job that we feel secure in but is not stimulating to us mentally. Realizing this does not mean we must find a new job. We may be able to improve on our present job without leaving it.

Part of what stops us from feeling our dissatisfactions too acutely is the fear of having to look for a new job. That idea may be terrifying enough that we keep plodding along, complaining now and then, but not looking too far to the right or left. What if we really took permission to feel our desires? If you wrote a list of all that you wanted in a job, how long would it be? If a friend agreed that you deserved this much, and even a little more, could you think of another "something" that's not quite right in your work?

Let's take a look at what those particulars might be. Some wishes might be for another break in the day, fewer deadlines to meet, more work to do that feels valuable, a longer lunch break, fewer rules, more social gatherings with co-workers, or someone to talk to about work stresses. Any of these are valid wishes.

When we don't have what we'd really like, chances are we have remained silent or nonpersistent because of our issues with visibility, personal worth, or power. But if we realize we really would want our job to be more enjoyable, more worthwhile, or better-paying, just admitting this can be the most difficult step. If you like, you can write one or more of them down on a piece of paper. Can you think of a solution that would help you feel better about your job? Can you also think of a second and third compromise that would at least help somewhat?

For example, how do we proceed if we would like to be paid more for what we do? To consider the options, we need to ignore how well or poorly the company is doing financially, or how much we "need" the money to pay more bills. We are only concentrating on the quality of the work we perform.

Reinforcing Our Self-Esteem

First of all, have you worked harder lately or taken on additional responsibilities? Write any of these down. Have you done something new that is saving the company money? Have you introduced something different that is bringing in more clients and new revenue? No matter how small a change it is, it may have dramatic effects.

If you haven't done any of these yet, can you think of any ideas about how you could do them? Brainstorm for a few minutes.

Another good reason to ask for a raise is that you have been doing your job for a while and your efficiency has improved, increasing your work output. Try thinking of other concrete ways which support your increased feelings of worth and confidence.

Next, determine what kind of raise you would like to have. Then figure out two more amounts that would be compromises but would still be better than what you are receiving now. These raises can be hourly or salary changes, increased paid vacation, or they might involve an idea you have about bonuses that could be awarded for completing a certain new kind of work.

In any compartment of our lives, when we voice a dissatisfaction along with a solution, it frees the listener from problem-solving so he or she can hear our solution more clearly. This can be true in our friendships and love relationships as well as our work. Living with dead-end complaints is draining for everybody, and it keeps us feeling victimized by our employers. However, when we use our creativity to find solutions, it stimulates interest in our work environment, and our involvement and actions help us feel more powerful again. It also gains the respect of others.

Changes Worth Trying
- ★ Rearrange your work station so everything is placed in its most efficient position.
- ★ If you are in personal conflict with a co-worker, get out a journal and express in writing how you really feel about your situation.

- ★ At the place where you volunteer, identify and suggest a change that you feel would help the workers do their job better.
- ★ Revise your resume. If you're not sure about its format or how to improve it, visit a library and consult the books there that cover constructing a resume.
- ★ Talk over your job stresses with your spouse or a friend.
- ★ Scan the classified ads in a newspaper to see if the wages advertised for a position similar to yours correspond to the salary you receive.
- ★★ When you are overburdened by work, ask for assistance from your boss or co-worker.
- ★★ Notice any repetitious jobs you do that could be done by a reasonably-priced office product or machine. Suggest its purchase.
- ★★ When the date for your review approaches, confirm with your employer which day it will occur.
- ★★ Notice when a posted list or documented requests would prevent crisscrossed and

confused verbal communications. Suggest it to your employer.

★★ If your co-worker is humming or making other sounds that are bothering you, say you are having trouble concentrating and ask if he or she could be a little quieter.

★★ Ask to, or without approval if you are able, rearrange parts of the common work space so they work better for everyone.

★★ When you see a need, create a position or a specific title for a particular set of duties. Write a proposal for it and send it through channels.

★★ If cigarette smoking is allowed in certain areas that you would frequent but don't because the smoke bothers you, see if you can think of another smoking area as an alternative. Suggest a change.

★★ If your company supports an employee assistance program, find out what your benefits are. Take advantage of the counselor's skills offered.

★★★ If you feel you have done a particularly outstanding job in recent months, identify the ways in which your work is boosting company morale or income. Ask that an extra review be performed.

★★★ Think of a raise amount you would feel really good about that would increase your feeling of worth to the company and strengthen your loyalty to the company as well. Ask for it, even if it's larger than you've ever asked for before.

★★★ If difficulties with child care continue to hamper your work ability in some way, see if you can find out what on-site day care costs are for other companies, and discuss with the appropriate personnel its feasibility for a company the size of yours.

★★★ Introduce a new bonus system idea to your boss.

It's natural to feel disappointed if one set of solutions doesn't work with an employer, but try not to let it sway you from your goal. Take time to feel good about having taken the risk! Then, when you're ready, try again with a new set of solutions. Keep cultivating the special feeling that you deserve a satisfying daily work life. And if in the end you decide you deserve more than this job can offer you, this is a compliment from yourself. These are concrete signs of your increasing generosity toward yourself.

I deserve to feel proud of my work.

13

Major Life Changes

Every step, even a tentative one, counts.

Anne Morrow Lindbergh

What Scares Us About Change?

Of all the topics in this book, that of major life changes is perhaps the most frightening. When we think in a black-and-white way, we forget that we don't have to attack an issue and solve it all at once. This chapter is not designed to get us to leave our home, quit our job, or break up with our partner. It is more about clearing our minds so we can see what suits us best, which may include finding that what we already have fits us perfectly.

Life changes are the largest ones we can make. Their magnitude is partly what frightens us. We avoid thinking about them because of this, or because someone we know is telling us we should change. We might be unsure how to proceed. We may not enjoy the unpredictability and insecurity of the unknown. We fear that a decision to change will be set in stone even if the decision ends up producing undesirable results. And we know we would have to reckon with a period of adjustment if we made a change.

Any of these factors is enough to stop us in our tracks. Since it is our avoidance of these issues and its resulting shame that tends to burden us, a good place to start exploring is in the area of postponement itself. What other components of avoidance are there? Perhaps we hear "shoulds" echoing somewhere in our mind. They may be saying that we should have already been thinking about these things, we should be solving the questions, and we should move on more easily. These "shoulds" make us feel ashamed and inept. But until we recognize them, we automatically react by turning away from them.

A First Step

How can we make life changes seem more approachable? One way is to look at other less dramatic areas of our lives that we are also postponing action on. One of those topics is chores we are putting off. Here's an exercise that may make all of these topics more approachable. Our goal will be to sweep out our minds and let a piece of paper be the receptacle. First, collect a blank piece of paper or two and a pencil. Write the heading "Life Change Questions I Don't Want to Think About." Under this write one or two questions like, "Am I best off in this job?", "Is this the climate I want to live in for the rest of my life?", "Does my love relationship need cleaning up or even clearing out?", "Would a new city have more to offer me?", "Am I unsatisfied with my current friendships but afraid of the prospect of being alone?" or, "Should I be in a different apartment?" Write down any that bother you or have an anxious charge.

It is worth noting that an anxious charge is merely a sign of inner conflict. Part of us wants to stay right where we are for security reasons, and part of us hints at something a little better awaiting us. We often remain still out of fear that the guiding voice will coerce us into doing what it advises if we listen to it, so we strive not to recognize it at all. Our conflict lessens when we remember we can choose to listen to these opposing voices while taking no action at all.

As the second part of the exercise, write a new heading called, "Chores I Don't Want to Do Today." Include regular chores you need to get done but don't particularly feel like doing, such as laundry, grocery shopping, mopping, or cleaning the toilet. Finally, write a third heading called, "Jobs I Don't Like to Get Around To." These items are less urgent or lengthy tasks you've been putting off, like sewing a button onto a shirt, taking the car in for maintenance, painting the house trim, defrosting the freezer, or writing letters. Take a little time to write these down so they'll stop niggling at the back of your mind.

With this completed, you have a couple of choices. You can put the piece of paper away. This leaves you free to concentrate on what you want to do. Sometimes we need to feel liberated from "shoulds." When we learn how to nurture and fulfill ourselves by doing fun things, we later feel more naturally able to choose and accomplish some of our less desirable tasks.

Another choice is to look at the last two lists you made. Without committing yourself to doing a task, ask yourself if there's an item you could see yourself doing. If one looks a bit more tantalizing than the rest, simply make a mark next to it and file the paper away.

Within a month refer back to this piece of paper. You may be surprised. You may have already accomplished a few of the tasks and you may also now realize they required relatively little effort to finish. Cross off any items you've completed.

It can be a relief just to identify preferences like these. In fact, it's a good idea to write lists like these periodically and then put them away. They remind us it's okay to clarify conflicts and state preferences. They remind us it's acceptable to take breaks from tasks now and then. It's also okay to realize how many tasks we do that we dislike, and that we can ask for help from our partner or a friend.

If you want to delve a little further into the life change topic you selected, you can start with a fresh piece of paper and write the title, "What I'm Afraid Of." These would be ideas such as "I'd be afraid I'd have to start taking steps faster than I was ready to," "I might have to accept something that's even worse than I have now," "I wouldn't know how to figure out the best way to proceed," "If I don't like where I am now, I wouldn't be able to trust my decision-making process next time," or, "I'm afraid of having something better." After "containing" doubts by verbalizing them, you may find that you can see your way to your next most comfortable step.

Celebrate Your Successes!

Already you have progressed. You have taken a look at things that are difficult to see because of the cloud of feelings that surround them. Be sure to acknowledge any sense of pride that comes up after doing these or any other tasks that are difficult. This feeling of pride is natural. Its size can be surprising. Since we don't often feel so happy with ourselves, take a moment or a half-day and bask in it. It is part of the reward, and part of the budding confidence that assists us into the present-day world. It helps us realize that taking the risk was worth every minute.

If you like, you can set up a task-and-reward date with yourself. Pick a time, such as fifteen minutes on Wednesday evening, to spend considering different aspects of a certain life change you feel anxious about. Arrange ahead of time to have an activity ready as a reward for accomplishing the fifteen minutes of thinking or writing. Relax by getting out some art supplies to play with, doing some aerobic exercise with a friend, or calling somebody long-distance you haven't spoken to in quite some time.

Making Changes

Following are some ideas that can help us adapt to the idea of making a life change.

- Plant a new tree in your yard or put up a bird feeder near your kitchen window.
- Even if you're not looking for a new job, look through the classified ads.
- If entering your home doesn't soothe or please you, find ways to make it suit you better. Move the furniture around, add a dimmer switch, change the air temperature or odor, or put a few pictures on the walls.
- Take an hour today just to play.
- Plan for remodeling a part of your home. Or start smaller by experimenting with curtains, rugs, paint, or mirrors to make it a cheerier place to be.
- Nourish your desire to have a new home, job, friend, lover, etc., by openly acknowledging to yourself how much you want one.
- Write a journal entry recognizing how frightened you feel about leaving secure ways of living behind, or how lost you feel about not yet having anything new to replace them with.

- ★ Paste together a collage with magazine pictures that shows where you want to be in your life and what you want to have for yourself.
- ★★ Make a mental note of the ways your rental apartment doesn't satisfy you. In your next apartment search, look for a better situation.
- ★★ Say no to the invitation of an acquaintance you'd rather not choose for a friend.
- ★★ Plan a vacation to an area with a climate you enjoy.
- ★★ Think of a few ways a new neighborhood or city would suit you better. Just for fun, go to a library that carries resourceful books like, *Places Rated Almanac* that list the pros and cons of your city and others nationwide.
- ★★ Think of a new acquaintance you like and invite him or her to do something with you.
- ★★ Write a list of what scares you about considering having a lover. Write another list

of what attracts you. Without acting any further on it, see if you can say to yourself with conviction that you are ready to have a partner to share with. If not, don't fret about it. If so, holding this conviction in your mind can be a first step.

★★ Find a way to volunteer in an area you've wanted to try.

★★ To make space for change in your life, start with your closets. Consider removing clothes that you don't wear or don't like anymore and bagging them for a garage sale or second-hand store.

★★★ Make a few plans, even if they are a year or more down the road, to move to a different area you think you'd enjoy more.

★★★ Review the relationships in your life. If you realize that some are abusive or unsupportive of your growth, consider confronting or not continuing with one friend or family member.

★★★ Send your resume out to places you might like to work.

- ★★★ When someone asks you out on a date and you're thinking of going mostly to escape loneliness, try declining.
- ★★★ If you have a romantic interest in someone, invite them out.

Any risk too large naturally scares us. With practice, we learn to recognize when we are in avoidance about something in our lives. In the shadow of any healthy risk stands a potential pleasure. When we divide the risk into smaller portions, the pleasure reappears, beckoning to us like pleasures naturally do. A risk is not unlike a watermelon: neither of them can really be enjoyed until they are cut into manageable slices.

I'm a success when I make a positive life change.

14

Prosperity and Deservedness

There wouldn't be such a thing as counterfeit gold if there were no real gold somewhere.

Old Sufi Proverb

Our Birthrights

What are we worthy of, after all? Throughout our lives, deservedness has been another of our murky issues. We were taught we had only the rights of a doll under the hands of our perpetrator, and no child in the world deserves that kind of treatment. It is our birthright to be loved and loving human beings. Where once we were not allowed to find our way, we now have the ability to look for and discover our purposes and joys, and we have the right to own them and bring them with us. Our sense of deservedness may have increased since we began reading this book. When we accept how we feel and enjoy how we think, we can grow into our potential.

Prosperity happens for us in different ways. It starts when we feel more generous and loving towards ourselves. Sometimes it can mean forgiving ourselves, perhaps for having felt compelled to hold certain mistaken beliefs for so long. And sometimes when we are busy with our own self-fulfillment, forgiveness of others also occurs. Prosperity comes with discovering our own complex richness and feeling comfortable owning our feelings, regardless of what they are and what is happening outside us.

As we dare to feel prosperous, we may start to ask a little more from life. Since we are investing our time and energy toward change, it is natural to feel more worthy, powerful, and purposeful. And since we are finding out more about our feelings, we can now afford to know what makes us feel happy.

In our culture, financial well-being is the primary way many people define prosperity. While earning, collecting, and using money are skills to be learned and respected, finances are only a small part of it. We can feel rich when we sense a spiritual connection with others, or an affinity with whatever seems divine to us. Feeling wealthy means we have friends we enjoy, music we feel touched by, and physical energy that increases as we find our life purposes. We begin to feel rich while baking cookies to eat with the kids next door, sitting down at a pottery project, or taking pride in a newly organized desktop. A feeling of abundance comes when we enjoy our small moments.

Self-Generosity and Forgiveness

While the idea of claiming a moment or two for ourselves in the course of each day seems manageable, the connection of self-generosity to forgiveness may be more perplexing. And it's no wonder, since at times we are bombarded with others' agendas about forgiveness. There are some who will tell us we can't go on without forgiving those who hurt us. Our culture and various religions pressure us to forgive and forget. However, this is neither helpful nor realistic.

First of all, forgiveness is not to be forced. It is *for giving*. If we have to whitewash our feelings to forgive someone, we risk burying ourselves again for the sake of someone else. We risk being victimized by a society that would like to keep the lid on incest. Secondly, forgiving our perpetrators never pardons or excuses their actions. No matter what, their actions were wrong. It is also important to remember that forgiveness moves only the forgiver, not the forgiven.

It is much less important to hold forgiveness as a goal than to focus on feeling each of the many emotions we are discovering. Forgiveness is a side-effect that naturally occurs when we continue to grow and learn.

What does forgiveness look or feel like, then? If it comes, it will be when we realize our anger and tears resulting from the incest are mostly spent. It will be when we no longer feel the shame and isolation and fear we have felt for many years. We will find we can acknowledge that our perpetrator was not perfect but was human and made mistakes. Our incest issues will be, in large part, in resolution, and we will find ourselves moving on to different phases of growth.

What about forgiving ourselves? Feeling more deserving means anything from doing a favor for ourselves to practicing a self-forgiving attitude. Forgiving ourselves does not imply that we ever did anything as wrong as our perpetrator did. It can mean we have more compassion about the ways we sometimes act out on ourselves. We learned to feel harsh against ourselves. Now we are beginning to understand that we can feel tenderness for both our rejecting, judgmental part and the child part that has felt rejected. We can give her our kindest attention because she was convinced nobody would ever come to find her. And we can invite him onto our lap and wrap our arms around him when he is too frightened to speak.

Striking It Rich

Following are some other ways that can help us expand our feelings of personal deserving and abundance.

- ★ Give yourself more attention by crawling into bed one night an hour early to watch a movie or have some solitude.

- ★ To improve your nearby environment, take a bag some afternoon and pick up garbage in your neighborhood.
- ★ Keep a few notebook pages free for ideas you might be able to sell one day, like ideas for an invention, new fashion concepts, or comic strip cartoons.
- ★ Practice not putting yourself down, or rebuffing compliments.
- ★★ Take a creative look at your budget. Figure out a way to save a few dollars this month and spend that money on a gift for yourself.
- ★★ Ask some friends to go with you to a sauna or whirlpool for an hour or two.
- ★★ Think of something major you've wanted all your life that has seemed out-of-reach because of its expense. Set up a separate bank account and deposit a regular amount of money each month toward your goal.
- ★★ Consider getting a pet you've wanted.

- ★★ Write down ten pleasures you enjoy. Then think of a way you could earn $50 in the next week or two by doing one of these things.
- ★★ Actively seek out one new friend.
- ★★ When buying a product, buy a model that's a step up from what you're used to.
- ★★★ Ask your partner ahead of time to tend to the children and the phone one morning so you can sleep late.
- ★★★ Volunteer a little time to be a rocker for newborn babies at a hospital, or a Big Brother or Big Sister to a child who is looking for one.
- ★★★ Plan a getaway weekend at a bed and breakfast inn with your partner.
- ★★★ Make an appointment with a masseur or masseuse to have some soothing body work done.
- ★★★ Ask your partner for assistance in arranging things you most want to do on your birthday.

With practice we learn how to attend to our child self. We learn when to listen, when to give a hug, when to write him a valentine, and when to surround her with teddy bears. Giving loving acceptance to all our feelings also allows us to discover our new excitement, hope, and pleasure and we find we are able to generate new tools for living that support our dedication to growth.

I feel healthy, rich, and creative.

15

Today and Tomorrow

*If I keep a green bough in my heart,
the singing bird will come.*

Chinese Proverb

Many incest victims and survivors in past generations lived and died so quietly that we don't even know who they were. Nor do we know if they had the potential to make creative contributions but were never able to.

In finding our way, we are growing beyond anonymity by at last becoming acquainted with ourselves. Some years ago an 81-year-old Kentucky woman wrote a piece about some secrets she'd discovered: her own joys and desires. While widely reprinted, hers is a message that bears repeating. It is child-like in its humor and wise in its self-acceptance, and it's a wonderful reminder about living in the moment and in the body.

If I Had My Life to Live Over

I'd like to make more mistakes next time. I'd relax, I would limber up. I would be sillier than I have been this trip. I would take fewer things seriously. I would take more chances. I would climb more mountains and swim more rivers. I would eat more ice cream and less beans. I would perhaps have more actual troubles, but I'd have fewer imaginary ones.

You see, I'm one of those people who live sensibly and sanely hour after hour, day after day. Oh, I've had my moments, and if I had it to do over again, I'd have more of them. In fact, I'd try to have nothing else. Just moments, one after another, instead of living so many years ahead of each day. I've been one of those persons who never goes anywhere without a thermometer, a hot water bottle, a raincoat, and a parachute. If I had to do it again, I would travel lighter than I have.

By expanding our horizons, we have nothing to lose but our fear, grief, and disappointment. We are learning to touch life itself. We remember feeling the stillness of this morning, we're mesmerized by trickling water in a creek, and we can finally hear the music of the singing bird.

However we are growing is right. As we strengthen the bonds inside ourselves, we recognize others like us. We feel them join hands with us to watch our storm clouds clear, to drink in the deep blue beyond. We make an ever-widening circle under an ever-widening sky.

Appendix A

What Might Have Happened?

While it is normal to feel disillusioned at times about our progress, it can be enlightening to realize how well we actually are doing. In truth, the "age of darkness" mentioned in Chapter One never succeeded in destroying our spirit. Indeed, we might wonder, why didn't any of these things happen instead?

With all the traumatic things that happened to me, how did I ever manage to keep breathing through it all?

Why didn't I give up?

Why didn't I try suicide more often, or more effectively?

Why didn't I end up hospitalized more?

Why didn't I stay in my addictions?

Why am I not completely insane?

How did I keep from being jailed for not knowing how to operate in this society?

How did I keep myself from being homeless?

How did I manage not to murder everyone who hurt me?

Why don't I have anxiety attacks every day?

How did I learn to function at all?

Why have I ever wanted a lover?

How could I ever consider masturbating?

How did I keep hope alive that anything, including this book, could make a difference in my life?

It is important to realize that we cultivated some kind of intelligence or clarity that helped us evolve from the darkest places of our abuse. We hear nowadays that as survivors we deserve a lot of credit. Whether or not you feel proud of being an incest survivor as opposed to one of the "incest crazy," or another "incest suicide," know this: the fact that you found ways to stay alive in an abusive atmosphere shows you have the creativity and strength to thrive in what is now a safer world.

Appendix B

Traps to Watch For

As we begin to ask new questions like those in Chapter Two about ourselves and our behaviors, we may bump into stumbling blocks. Anyone stumbles from time to time, but a survivor trying new risks will encounter pitfalls specific to incest. These were reinforced in many ways until we believed them. However, they are lies. Their purpose is to protect the secret of incest by preventing the survivor from growing. Identify any others you are familiar with.

1) You can't win!
2) You are inadequate. You won't succeed.
3) You are crazy to try changing.
4) You can't know yourself well enough to get out of this.
5) You'll hurt someone by breaking the silence.
6) You have more power than anybody else (and you better not screw it up).

7) You might feel good now, but bad is sure to follow.
8) You have to stay in pieces and unfeeling or you won't make it.
9) Closeness is dangerous.
10) Why try? It never worked before.

As you strengthen yourself, these pitfalls will disempower you less and less. We absorbed enough programming to last a lifetime. After all, the incest in our families most likely has already lasted several generations. We will never know how many of our relatives tried and failed to break out of the abuse before us. It may be useful to make up a personal motto, like "I will not pass it on," or, "The buck stops with me!"

Appendix C

Am I the Only One?

To shed more light on some of the secret beliefs you may have about Chapter Eleven's subject of sex and intimacy, let's try identifying them. Many of us may actually share the same beliefs.

If you have ever had sexual experiences with others, or are currently in a love relationship, see if you can recall ever having had any of these thoughts.

I am the only one who:

   . . . is this bad as a lover.
   . . . has such a low sex drive.
   . . . wishes sex weren't a part of life.
   . . . thinks my partner would freak out if I revealed that sometimes she or he resembles my perpetrator.
   . . . hates sex almost all the time.

. . . can't bring myself to say no because my partner would leave me.
. . . is the most quiet lover anywhere.
. . . leaves my body during lovemaking.
. . . is a bad lover because my partner likes certain things I can hardly think about, let alone participate in.
. . . feels silly when I still need a light off or on, or a door closed or open while lovemaking.
. . . is paralyzed into silence, especially when sex is not working for me.
. . . wishes my partner would simply know how to satisfy me and I wouldn't have to say anything.
. . . thinks if I say no I'm being unreasonable.
. . . thinks if I start saying no I'll never stop.
. . . is unsensual. I could never touch someone in a way that would make them desire me.
. . . is such an unwilling lover.

- . . . thinks my lover is only pretending to enjoy sex with me.
- . . . thinks my lover secretly would rather be with someone who has no sexual issues.
- . . . feels like a big inconvenience to my partner.
- . . . hates being asked during lovemaking to stimulate my partner a little differently.
- . . . feels trapped by the mere thought of being in a relationship.
- . . . feels ugly sexually.
- . . . can't feel certain body parts during lovemaking.
- . . . doesn't know what my sexuality means to me.
- . . . thinks I'll never get over my stumbling blocks.
- . . . feels shame when making love.
- . . . worries that lovemaking will always be an uncomfortable and anxious experience.

Much of the time we feel sure we are poor lovers. It would be sad if this were a permanent attitude, but fortunately it doesn't have to be. With increasing awareness of ourselves, we can transform sex into a new playtime—frolicsome and uninhibited and pleasurable for us.

Appendix D

What *Do* I Feel During Sex?

To further shed some of the shame we feel around the sexual issues mentioned in Chapter Eleven, it is helpful to identify how we feel when making love. We might be able to identify, for example, a kind of numbness or vacancy, but if we really explore the specific sensations we feel during sexual play, what do we find?

My hands don't like to move around or be too expressive.

My arms don't feel like hugging my partner.

I think of doing the laundry or shopping.

I have a repulsed feeling in my crotch.

I think this is the worst part of relationships.

My skin doesn't feel alive.

I can watch both of us from outside myself.

I try to hurry things along so they'll be done faster.

My legs want to cross and stay that way.

I can't bear to show I'm aroused.

My lips feel numb.

I am repulsed by seeing my partner nude.

I feel ashamed when my partner sees me naked.

I can't bring myself to say sexy things.

I feel too vulnerable to have an orgasm so I keep myself away from the arousal I could feel.

I worry my partner will be bored with me.

When I try to re-enter my body, I can't.

I want to say something but I feel totally paralyzed.

I worry I'll take too long before having an orgasm.

I feel like a failure most of the time.

I wonder if I'll ever be able to have an orgasm with my partner.

I act the same as always sexually, and it might not be exciting, but I feel paralyzed about trying new techniques.

I feel a spotlight shining on me when I am "performing" as a lover.

Sometimes just identifying these feelings helps us feel lighter about the subject of sex. It may also help us if we communicate these feelings to our partner. In the end, the more honest we are with ourselves, the more we are able to clear away the cobwebs and see sex for what it can be, an opportunity for intimacy where both partners feel understood, loved, and appreciated for who they are.

Postscript

If you would like to share any feedback with the author, feel free to send your letter to:

Parkside Publishing Corporation
ATTN: The Singing Bird Will Come
205 W. Touhy Avenue
Park Ridge, Illinois 60068-5881

All letters will be forwarded unopened and in confidence to the author.